Reporting from the Danger Zone

D0713945

Journalism is a dangerous business when one's "beat" is a war-zone, a corrupt regime, or organized crime. In *Reporting from the Danger Zone*, Maria Armoudian reveals the complications facing frontline journalists who cover these hotspots, including how they find, access, and deliver their stories while keeping themselves safe from harm.

Although conflict journalism has always been fraught with danger, today's reporters face even more perilous conditions while also contending with shrinking journalism budgets, news outlets' greater reliance on free-lancers, tracking technologies, and increasingly hostile terrain. Armoudian also contrasts the difficulties of foreign correspondents who navigate alien sources, languages, and land, with domestically situated war correspondents who witness their own homelands being torn apart.

Armoudian documents journalists' thoughts, emotions, and strategies in their own words. Their dramatic and compelling journeys reveal the fortitudes and frailties of humanity as well as the dynamics and struggles of the information wars, revealing factors that determine the information we do, and do not, receive from danger zones.

Maria Armoudian is a Lecturer in Media and Politics at the University of Auckland. She is the author of *Kill the Messenger: Media's Role in the Fate of the World* (2011).

Reporting from the Danger Zone

Frontline Journalists, Their Jobs, and an Increasingly Perilous Future

Maria Armoudian

Routledge
Taylor & Francis Group

NEW YORK AND LONDON

First published 2017
by Routledge
711 Third Avenue, New York, NY 10017

and by Routledge
2 Park Square, Milton Park, Abingdon, Oxon OX14 4RN

Routledge is an imprint of the Taylor & Francis Group, an informa business

© 2017 Taylor & Francis

Library of Congress Cataloging in Publication Data
Names: Armoudian, Maria, author.
Title: Reporting from the danger zone : frontline journalists, their jobs, and an increasingly perilous future / Maria Armoudian.
Description: New York : Routledge, 2016. | Includes index.
Identifiers: LCCN 2016005687| ISBN 9781138840041 (hardback) | ISBN 9781138840058 (pbk.) | ISBN 9781315733067 (ebk.)
Subjects: LCSH: Journalism--Vocational guidance. | Reporters and reporting--Vocational guidance. | Foreign news.
Classification: LCC PN4888.F69 A76 2016 | DDC 071/.3023--dc23
LC record available at http://lccn.loc.gov/2016005687

ISBN: 978-1-138-84004-1 (hbk)
ISBN: 978-1-138-84005-8 (pbk)
ISBN: 978-1-315-73306-7 (ebk)

Typeset in Goudy
by Taylor & Francis Books

Printed and bound in the United States of America by Publishers Graphics, LLC on sustainably sourced paper.

For Dr. Garabed Armoudian, for immeasurable guidance and support

Contents

Acknowledgments

It is always an impossible task to thank everyone who had a role to play in my being able to write this book. Many thanks to my institution, the University of Auckland, which funded this project through a grant from the Faculty Research Development Fund.

The research for this book relied upon interviews with 32 journalists who took time out of their extremely busy days to share their thoughts and experiences. Thank you Mae Azango, Umar Cheema, John Dinges, Andrew Glazer, Danny Gold, Roy Gutman, Dahr Jamail, Kemal Kurspahic, Allan Little, Terry McCarthy, Eamonn McCann, Martin McGinley, David McKittrick, Terry McLaughlin, Eamonn Mallie, Jason Mojica, Michael Parks, Sandra Rodriguez Nieto, David Schlesinger, Jon Stephenson, Balint Szlanko, Andreii Vovk, Carol Williams, and Bob Woodruff. Also, the journalists who asked to remain anonymous, including C11, IJ1, IJ2, IJ7, PC10, and PJ09.

I owe the biggest debt of gratitude to Bernard Duncan for the day-in-day-out consultation on this project.

Thank you to Corazon Miller, Sam Smith, Paul Karon, and Kate Svyatets whose help with research, wordsmithing, transcripts, and translation were indispensable.

And to my supportive colleagues in my department, Politics and International Relations, Barry Milne at Compass, and throughout the School of Arts (especially Tim Page and Mike Hurst for above-and-beyond support).

For your ongoing encouragement through thick and thin, thank you to my family, my parents, Dr. Garabed and Aghavni Armoudian, and my dear friends, Ankine Aghassian, Wyatt Underwood, Dutch Stowe, Charles "Kit" Crittenden, and Denise Robb.

I will always owe a debt of gratitude to my colleagues and mentors at my previous institutions—the University of Southern California, especially to Patrick James, Ann Crigler, Hrair Dekmejian, Ricardo Ramirez, Robert English, Ernest Wilson, and Phil Seib—and CSULA, especially Scott Bowman.

Writing a book such as *Reporting from the Danger Zone* heightens an author's senses as to the real issues facing those who struggle and risk to bring vital information to the world. We owe them much, and do well to recognize their courage and dedication.

1   Introduction

Why Ethical Journalism Matters

They were less than an hour south of the Turkish border. Freelance journalist James Foley, photojournalist John Cantlie and their translator stopped at a café in Northern Syria to transmit their reports. An hour later, the men hailed a taxi, climbed in, and headed north. They never made it. Masked gunmen in a van overtook the taxi's left side, forcing it to a halt. The gunmen screamed as they leapt from the van. They forced the two journalists to the ground, handcuffed them, and hauled them into captivity (Callimachi 2014). The abductors, members of the "Islamic State" (also ISIS or ISIL), who took over swaths of Syria and Iraq, tortured Foley with beatings, water-boarding, upside-down hanging, and mock executions, before publicly beheading him (ibid.).

Foley was the second of five journalists decapitated by an extremist group and one of the 1,185 journalists who have been killed on the job since 1992, according to the Committee to Protect Journalists (CPJ) (2016), which gathers data on attacks on journalists and media freedom. Although violence against journalists is not a new phenomenon, the trend has worsened. The year 2012, for example, saw a 33 percent rise in journalist slayings, according to Reporters sans frontiers (RSF) (Reporters without Borders 2012), 43 percent according to CPJ (2012, 2014). The death toll is accompanied by a 37 percent rise in abductions (to 119) between 2013 and 2014, notes the group (Reporters without Borders 2014). In addition to the abductions and deaths, hundreds more have been imprisoned or exiled (CPJ 2015). Local journalists bear the brunt of the violence and slayings, accounting for more than 75 percent of journalists killed and imprisoned, according to CPJ and RSF, the latter of which found 90 percent of journalist abductions were locals (Reporters without Borders 2014).

The attacks signal a dark era for journalism and a stark departure from previous decades when combatants, at minimum, tolerated journalists, treating them as civilians, and often sought their sympathies. Convincing journalists of "our" righteousness and "their" wrongness was part of the information wars[1] that run parallel to the physical wars. Rebels, freedom fighters, and others relied upon journalists to tell their stories, and relay their grievances and perspectives to the rest of the world in hopes of boosting their legitimacy, gaining international sympathies and persuading audiences of the virtues of their causes. The Irish Republican Army (IRA), for example (covered more in Chapter 5, "Living in a Danger Zone"), carefully crafted communication campaigns and cultivated relationships with local and international journalists to help win support for their cause (Armoudian 2011, 2013).

Many factors have changed the equation, among them, the internet. With new communication technologies, sophisticated fighters no longer need journalists to tell their stories, instead they disseminate their unfiltered messages and frames directly to the public, free from the check of independent journalism. And though the internet also gives voice to oppressed citizens to communicate outside of closed borders, it has simultaneously empowered groups such as the Islamic State to expand their reach to persuade and terrorize (see, for example, Klausen 2015).

In this new equation, journalists are part of the story, rather than conduits of stories. The harrowing public displays of their deaths are part of the information wars waged by extremists. Designed to horrify and terrify, gruesome public killings of correspondents capture attention, induce grief across the globe, and project a sick form of power. And alongside the rest of their campaigns, extremist groups such as the "Islamic State" persuade potential recruits to join their cause.

Simultaneously, they generate an eerie silence, as the rash of killings and kidnappings have persuaded journalists and their managers to opt out of covering dangerous territories and groups. After a dozen deaths just within the first 10 years of the twenty-first century, then Reuters Editor-in-Chief, David Schlesinger, called for a new, more cautious approach to danger zone journalism. "We have to say 'no' more often. We have to be prepared to miss the image more often. We have to be ready to lose the shot to avoid being shot. We must be ready to lose some stories to avoid losing yet more lives," he said (Schlesinger 2010).

During Schlesinger's leadership, after Reuters journalists Namir Noor-Eldeen and Saeed Chmagh were gunned down in Iraq by US Apache fighters, the company adopted a policy that journalists must not stand next to armed, non-uniformed persons. But Schlesinger argues the policy does not go far enough. He advocates that editors "should be opting to 'pass' on more stories more often," and instead rely upon "the great democratisation of technology." Simultaneously, he advocated for training, including similar avoidance, for local citizen journalists who blog and tweet and "might rush in to the very danger spots we should be avoiding" (ibid.).

Other news organizations are adopting related policies. Agence France Presse (AFP), for instance, stopped sending journalists into rebel-held parts of Syria, a region it deemed too risky to cover. "Journalists are no longer welcome in rebel-held Syria, as independent witnesses to the suffering of local populations. They have become targets, or commodities to be traded for ransom," declared its Global News Director (Léridon 2014).

Simultaneously, AFP sought to discourage freelance journalists from losing their lives by announcing that it would no longer accept any freelance journalists' work from those regions.

> We no longer accept work from freelance journalists who travel to places where we ourselves would not venture. It is a strong decision, and one that may not have been made clear enough, so I will repeat it here: if someone travels to Syria and offers us images or information when they return, we will not use it. Freelancers have paid a high price in the Syrian conflict. High enough. We will not encourage people to take that kind of risk.
>
> (ibid.)

The profession, its professionals, and those of us who rely upon them are at a crossroads. The threats add to an already encumbered institution, beleaguered by shrinking journalism budgets, dismantled foreign bureaus, and diminished foreign news coverage. Alongside long-term economic pressures, the trends further reduce the capacity of news organizations to deliver much-needed understandings about these developments.

What might the costs of avoidance and reduced coverage be? Can the costs be properly assessed? The absence of responsible journalism can have broad effects. As I wrote in my previous book, *Kill the Messenger: The Media's Role in the Fate of the World*, extremist control of information and framing aided the twentieth century's worst atrocities, including the Rwandan Genocide, the Nazi Holocaust, and the Bosnian War. Genocidal leaders used mass media to disseminate Blame Frames, Hate Frames, and Genocidal Frames to justify mass slaughters of innocent people as "solutions" for political problems and a means to achieve "noble" ends. These messages were weapons in the arsenal of the rhetorical wars, in aid of the physical wars of guns and bombs (Armoudian 2011). In Rwanda, Nazi Germany and parts of the former Yugoslavia, in the absence of ethical journalism, extremist ideas and frames went unchallenged and became the dominant narratives (ibid.).

Ethical journalists see through the frame wars. They seek to witness events, analyze developments, untangle truth from propaganda and provide nuanced understandings, ultimately countering extremist messages. At its best, responsible journalism impacts life and death by helping people better understand the complex realities of conflicts, informing their decisions with accurate, contextual information. They help policymakers prevent misinformed deadly errors. For these reasons and more, international conventions, news organizations and human rights groups seek to protect and expand media freedoms toward unfettered access to information (see, for example, Reporters without Borders 2015).

Pulitzer Prize-winning journalist and author Roy Gutman reiterated some consequences he reported in the book, *How We Missed the Story*: "If we [journalists] missed the story, then the literate readers, the educated citizens, and even the politicians, and those in power, leaders, missed the story," he explained. "Afghanistan was one of those places we [journalists] should have put on the map" (Gutman 2014).

Proper investigation of Afghanistan during the 1990s could have better informed and prepared decision-makers long before the 9/11 attacks, argued Gutman.

> So what are the consequences? You can't blame 9/11 on journalists. But you can say that the response, the very stupid response, the very unmeasured response and the excessive, wrong response by the Bush administration was aided by the fact that nobody knew what had happened prior to 9/11. Nobody had the narrative. Nobody understood the origins of Al Qaeda's grip on Afghanistan. And there's a hugely important gap, I thought, in people's knowledge of what preceded 9/11. And you need to know that in order to know how to really cope with these terror groups that now thrive and have now metastasized to other places, because the wrong response is not just counter-productive, but literally leads to the wrong thing.
>
> (ibid.)

Today, Gutman points to Syria where, again, informational black holes abound, and history threatens to repeat itself:

> So here we are. The biggest, most deadly war on earth where the most war crimes are occurring daily, where you have a regime basically going after civilians. And then you have the Islamic State, one of the most rapacious and extremist groups ever to be seen on the planet. And we are not going in and covering it ... Now people do get tired of wars. They go on for a long time, so it's hard to interest the public in something going on this long. But nevertheless there are ways. But not being there is not one of the ways. Not being there makes it infinitely harder.
>
> (ibid.)

This also goes some way to explain why journalists have become pawns in this real-life game of thrones. Obviously, killing journalists stops independent observation and prevents much analysis, knowledge of transgressions and dissemination of deeper understandings about complex issues arising in conflicts. It stops the check on propaganda, while their publicized murders also send a message of horror and power, chilling other potential observers—ultimately, the most extreme means of controlling information.

Extremist groups are just one of many players in the information wars. All war-makers use information and control of information as part of their arsenal in the battlefield of our hearts and minds. They restrict access; they "spin" and censor information, and they wage a war of ideas through their own media to persuade, entice, advocate, and project, as reflected by the markedly different reports that come from, for example, state-owned media such as RT, BBC, Al Jazeera or commercial media such as Bloomberg or CNN (see for example, Rodgers 2012). While reporting on the Ukraine conflict, veteran correspondent Carol Williams observed the phenomenon directly: "You get two diametrically opposed versions whether you're reading Russian media or whether you're reading Ukrainian media," she said. "There are just alternative realities that are unfolding there, according to the [respective] media" (Williams 2014).

Williams covered the conflict in Crimea, which she called "a good thing, because there were a lot of lies." But as the conflict spread, she said, "Nobody is covering everything" (ibid.).

Instead, with news organizations increasingly reluctant to send correspondents to the region, Williams and colleagues are left to a "kind of blogging and doing what I call 'the practice that used to be known as plagiarism.' I just feel really uncomfortable. Even though I've been to all these places, it's just not the same, rewriting about them and sourcing it to a Ukraine news agency," she said (ibid.).

In the age of diminished direct observation, the practice that discomforts Williams has ostensibly spread to other news agencies.

> I thought it was just *The LA Times* … But *The New York Times* has someone doing exactly what I'm doing. What they're relying on is the news media of the country where the event is unfolding. And they may not be as reliable and balanced and fair as I would be.
>
> (ibid.)

Despite advocating to avoid dangerous regions, Schlesinger acknowledges the looming problems, including misunderstandings arising from the inability of journalists to interview combatants, "That means that you never get a very full picture of the other side. You end up demonizing an entire people, and an entire movement because you don't actually get any of the nuance" (Schlesinger 2014).

Technology, however, has also filled some information gaps. While foreign news has diminished in the pages and broadcasts of traditional news organizations, information continues to flow, so much so that journalist and professor Michael Parks believes there is "more reporting done now" than when major newspapers had many remote bureaus. The difference today, he said, is "you just don't find it in your morning paper. You find it on your morning screen" (Parks 2014). In Syria, for example, he noted that he could "follow the war" with specialty websites.

> There is a website that follows attacks on women, very detailed— attacked, raped, whatever, abducted; Human Rights Watch, very

detailed reports; International Crisis Group, very detailed; citizen journalism … There's a ton of stuff. However, what you don't have is as many people attempting to integrate it and with the point of view of Americans' interests. You have to do it yourself.

(ibid.)

Through social media sites, such as Twitter, audiences "piece together" events as they happen, "instead of going to a news outlet," added Vice News Editor-in-Chief, Jason Mojica.

And [that's] not to say that a news outlet with a slower more methodical approach wouldn't have. I'm sure they ultimately did provide a cleaner, more accurate version of events. But I guess the difference is there was that immediacy. It's kind of the newspaper being yesterday's news versus being able to follow in real time what was happening.

(Mojica 2014)

Collectively a "powerful tool," social media brings additional problems, including unfiltered information, which translates to "It could be true or may not be true," noted Mojica (ibid.). This has created another challenge for danger zone journalism—verification (discussed more in Chapter 6, "The First Casualty").

This book, *Reporting from the Danger Zone*, explores some of these complications of danger zone journalism, how journalists deal with them, and how the job is changing. Based on more than 30 interviews with danger zone journalists past and present, it explores how journalists navigate obstacles in a changing global context to deliver the stories they believe are important. Through their stories, the book documents journalists' thoughts, emotions, decisions, and strategies related to fulfilling what most interviewees consider a duty to document the unfolding of history, expose iniquities, usually with the hope of helping alleviate suffering. Through retelling their journeys, we gather insight into the factors explaining the stories we do or do not receive in our daily supply of news.

The book reflects on some of these themes, primarily across four dimensions—past versus present danger-zone reporting, and local versus foreign coverage. Interviewees included foreign, local, and dual-identity journalists, the latter who report on their original countries, but as foreign correspondents based in another land. They include both men and women, both staffers and freelancers. They span several ethnicities and representatives from print, broadcast, and electronic journalism.

While there is remarkable common ground among most interviewed correspondents, important distinctions became evident between each of these groups and across particular hotspots of the world. Most interviewees, for example, shared a deep sense of duty and ethic, which alongside norms of journalism and their own emotions, guided their newsgathering. They expressed compassion for the afflicted, outrage toward perpetrators, and hope that their work would correct the iniquities. But distinct for local journalists, the professional was deeply personal: the suffering was among their own families, friends, and communities, and seeing this first-hand intensified their commitments to remain in the profession and in the danger zones in hopes of helping solve some of their countries' problems.

Chapter 2, "On the Origin of Stories," tells the stories about the stories from the danger zone, and how they came to be. It begins with the fundamental orientation of danger zone journalists, how this orientation leads them to choose and report one story over another, and how this manifests itself into our news. A blend of news norms, emotions, interests, beliefs, and values come together to send journalists into particular territories in search of the news to send back home.

In Chapter 3, "A Foreign Correspondent's Afflictions," through their own narratives, foreign correspondents expose a profession fraught with risks, hardships, traumas. The close-calls, abductions, and narrow escapes, the pain they witness, and the stress they endure affect the person and the profession both for positive and negative. For some, the experiences inure them. For others, they expand appreciation for the comforts at home. And still, some bear lifelong scars that impair their ability to continue with the same enthusiasm for their profession.

In Chapter 4, "Staying Alive," foreign correspondents discuss their strategies for maintaining safety and well-being. Changing circumstances have called for new measures, including for some, the decision to entirely forgo some territories and groups. But when they decide that the importance of the story outweighs the risk, foreign correspondents use a wide range of strategies to stay alive and well when entering, reporting, and exiting the danger zones.

Chapter 5, "Living in the Danger Zone," relates the real-life travails and triumphs of local journalists from Bosnia, Northern Ireland, Pakistan, Mexico, Liberia, and Russia. The chapter details local journalists' decisions, pursuits, and limitations while living in the danger zones. These journalists reveal their unique experiences while reporting on dangerous or taboo topics and reveal how their experiences, commitments, emotions, and professional goals differ from those of their foreign correspondent counterparts. Contrasting with both foreign correspondents and present-day local correspondents in the previous chapter, local journalists reveal how their histories, frustrations, emotions, and experiences shaped their stories and beyond.

Chapter 6, "The First Casualty," follows journalists' attempts to navigate through multiple obstacles in the way of accurate documentation about what they believe are important histories. It explores more deeply the changing nature of war and access, journalists' efforts to separate reality from bravado, spin, and pure fiction, and how they wrest their stories from the throes of censorship, whether from militaries or their own bosses. It includes their decisions about trade-offs related to embedding with militaries or independently sneaking into dangerous territories.

Chapter 7 brings these interviews together to draw their chief conclusions and fits them into the rich body of work by scholars and journalists who have already contributed to our understandings about journalism, journalists, and their roles in danger zones. Together, they offer broader lessons for ethical danger zone journalism.

Note

1 Information Wars is a phrase used by scholars such as Tumber and Webster (2006), though theirs takes a different meaning. I refer to this battle to persuade as a part of the totality of a war as a "rhetorical war" or "frame war" (Armoudian 2011, 2013). Liz Curtis (1984) called it a "Propaganda War" when detailing the communication during the Northern Ireland conflict.

References

Armoudian, Maria. 2011. *Kill the Messenger: The Media's Role in the Fate of the World*. Amherst, NY: Prometheus Books.

Armoudian, Maria. 2013. *The Politics of Transformation: Mass Media and the Northern Ireland Peace Process*. Ph.D. dissertation. University of Southern California.

Callimachi, Rukmini. 2014. "The Horror before the Beheadings." *The New York Times*. October 25.

Committee to Protect Journalists. 2012. "Journalist Deaths Spike in 2012 due to Syria, Somalia." December 18. https://www.cpj.org/reports/2012/12/journalist-deaths-spike-in-2012-due-to-syria-somal.php. Accessed March 28, 2016.

Committee to Protect Journalists. 2014. "61 Journalists Killed in 2012/Motive Confirmed." https://CPJ.org/killed/2014. Accessed March 28, 2016.

Committee to Protect Journalists. 2015. "Journalists Exiled." https://www.cpj.org/exile/. Accessed March 28, 2016.

Committee to Protect Journalists. 2015. "Journalists Imprisoned." https://www.cpj.org/imprisoned/2015.php. Accessed March 28, 2016.

Committee to Protect Journalists. 2016. "Journalists Killed since 1992." https://www.cpj.org/killed/. Accessed March 28, 2016.

Curtis, Liz. 1984. *Ireland and the Propaganda Wars: The British Media and the Battle for Hearts and Minds*. Concord, MA: Pluto Press.

Gutman, Roy. 2008. *How We Missed the Story: Osama bin Laden, the Taliban, and the Hijacking of Afghanistan*. Washington: United States Institute of Peace.

Gutman, Roy. 2014. Personal Interview. Via Skype. Auckland to Istanbul. December 6.

Klausen, Jytte. 2015. "Tweeting the Jihad: Social Media Networks of Western Foreign Fighters in Syria and Iraq." *Studies in Conflict & Terrorism*. 38:1, 1–22.

Léridon, Michèle 2014. "Covering the 'Islamic State'" http://blogs.afp.com/correspondent/?post%2Fcovering-the-islamic-state-afp#.VBshxi5YQU6. Agence France Presse. Accessed December 14, 2015.

Mojica, Jason. 2014. Personal Interview. In Person. Brooklyn, NY. October 31.

Parks, Michael. 2014. Personal Interview. In Person. Los Angeles. November 18.

Reporters Without Borders. 2012. https://en.rsf.org/press-freedom-barometer-journalists-killed.html?annee=2012. Accessed March 28, 2016.

Reporters Without Borders. 2014. "Round-Up of Abuses Against Journalists." https://en.rsf.org/files/bilan-2014-EN.pdf. Accessed March 28, 2016.

Reporters Without Borders. 2015. "RSF Hails Security Council's Historic Decision on Protecting Journalists." May 27. http://en.rsf.org/rsf-hails-security-council-s-27-05-2015,47939.html. Accessed December 15, 2015.

Rodgers, James. 2012. "The Air Raids that Never Were and the War that Nobody Won: Government Propaganda in Conflict Reporting and How Journalists Should Respond to it." *Global Media and Communication*. April. 9:1.

Schlesinger, David. 2010. Keynote Speech. "In Harm's Way." International News Safety Institute, November 10, Athens. http://dartcenter.org/content/in-midst-danger. Accessed December 8, 2015.

Schlesinger, David. 2014. Personal Interview. Via Skype. Auckland to Hong Kong. November 27.

Tumber, Howard, and Frank Webster. 2006. *Journalists under Fire: Information War and Journalistic Practices*. London & Thousand Oaks, CA: SAGE Publication.

Williams, Carol. 2014. Personal Interview. In Person. Los Angeles, CA. June 26.

2 On the Origin of Stories

Here's the big lesson from Afghanistan: The Taliban didn't want us there. Why? Just like the Serbs in 1992 in Bosnia. Why? Because they're up to no good. And if they're up to no good, that's where I want to be.

Roy Gutman, Pulitzer Prize-winning journalist (Gutman 2014)

It was a statement about the origin of stories: Gutman is on the job to expose wrongdoings. That job description—as an investigator—determines his jobsite, which in turn, shapes his stories and the times they are most vital—when institutions fail: "What the hell is a reporter doing revealing something in the heart of Europe that the CIA didn't spot? Or the International Red Cross did not sound an alarm on? Or the UN High Commission for Refugees? Or somebody else?" Gutman asked about his role in discovering concentration camps in Bosnia during the Yugoslav Wars (ibid.).

This indictment of institutions and their failures to uphold declared humanitarian laws and values encapsulates Gutman's view of the journalist's unique ethic and watchdog role. Though not universally held, this foundation—a fundamental set of values and a keen emotional sense of when these values are violated—is the origin of stories for many danger zone journalists. They are the last bastion of truth and accountability when others fail, an orientation evidenced by the seriousness and tenacity of interviewed journalists' pursuits. This orientation gives birth to some of the most important danger zone stories.

Long before war tore the Yugoslav federation into disparate states, Gutman had "fallen in love with Yugoslavia." But when he realized "the place that I knew and I thought I really loved had come apart," his love of the place, alongside a profound interest in human rights, impelled his return to the imperiled country (ibid.).

Initial rumors about atrocities—rape, concentration camps, and torture—were met with skepticism. But emerging details sounded alarm bells for Gutman. "There was a story about how the Serbs were deporting people from inside Bosnia in sealed trains, passenger trains. Then I heard about them doing it in freight cars, in their goods wagons," he said. "It was like step by step that I heard about this" (ibid.).

By way of Croatia, another clue emerged. "I had subscribed to one of the [Croatian] news agencies because I thought that I might learn something from it. And I read some accounts by people who said that they had seen concentration camps, and I decided that was true. I didn't know how I could prove it, but I decided that it just rang true," he explained (ibid.).

Another warning sign—a media lockout on the part of the Serb-led government—automatically evoked a sense that "something terrible is going on inside. [But] you don't know what" (ibid.).

Determined to find out, Gutman began his journey, querying opposition parties before approaching the government. Accompanied by a photographer from East Germany and a local Serb reporter and translator, he headed to Serbia's capital, Belgrade, then made the trek to the outskirts of Banja Luka, a suspected concentration camp in Bosnia-Herzegovina. "We were the first reporters there in Banja Luka to make it on the corridor," he said, describing it as "one of those horrible trips, 15 hours, and you were going through battle zones, and you didn't get to sleep [and] had to sleep on the floor. There were no hotels. It was not a fun trip" (ibid.).

Though moving away from "the main theater of war" seemed counterintuitive, Gutman believed that the key to understanding the politics of the capital lay in investigating the provinces. "I felt that the Serbs knew they could distract our attention by the siege of Sarajevo," he said. "And what they were really up to was happening in places where reporters were not going. So that led me to try there ... where they don't want us or where they're trying to direct us against, away from ... The only thing that was happening [in Sarajevo] was that it was being shot at, whereas the torture and killing of innocent civilians was going on, for the most part, way out of camera range, going on in the north" (ibid.).

Based on knowledge from past assignments, Gutman nudged officials more than usual. "Having known how the military worked there [and] having had good relations with them in my previous time, I just decided I can ask them to do things [that in] most places I would never ask them to do," he said (ibid.).

His strategy? Gutman assured the Serb leadership that he could dispel rumors of abuse and torture if he could witness for himself that they were false. "They thought about it, and they said, 'Okay, come back tomorrow at nine, and we'll go to one of the camps'" (ibid.).

With a final stop at the International Committee of the Red Cross (IRC), Gutman would be ready to attend the camp the next morning. The IRC staff, too, had plans to see the camp known as Manjaca. But they discouraged Gutman from attending at the same time. "They were hoping not to see me there because it got right in the way of their work," he said. "They really don't like to talk to the media in general" (ibid.).

The next morning at Manjaca, the IRC staff called for Gutman's removal. "[They] said, 'Will you get this journalist out of here?' And the

Serbs said, 'No, we want him to witness everything that we're doing and how open we are with you.' So [it was] one of those really unusual encounters where you're being used by the authorities to put across their version of events and what a happy smiling place it is," recalled Gutman. "And the Serbs, they put on a show for them and for me. And in fact the Serbs were happy to have me there because as I was questioning prisoners, who they'd lined up for me to talk to, they were filming me, and it was obviously going to be on the nightly news" (ibid.).

Their "official" version of things would soon be proven untrue. In the distance, Gutman's photographer observed what he believed signaled trouble. "He could spot degradation. He could spot that people, prisoners were being lined up to have their heads shaved like sheep with big sheep shearers," recalled Gutman. "And he knew that that picture was the summing up of everything that was going on there" (ibid.).

It was the first trickling evidence that the Serb government was running camps. "Now this was not a concentration camp in the sense where they were beating everybody and killing them daily. But people were dying of starvation, of malnutrition, of illness, untreated illness," said Gutman. "They were kept in big barns that were built as an army farm, if you can believe it ... [and] I wrote about that place, Manjaca, as sort of a holding zone for males" (ibid.).

Gutman's next target was another camp rumored to be much worse. "The place I wanted to go to was Omarska because there I'd heard that people were being killed daily in significant numbers and that it really was a concentration camp. [Originally] the military guys ... said they would take me, but then they changed their mind. They warned me that my security could not be assured. They offered to take me to other places," recalled Gutman, adding, "I was going through immense frustration because I felt we [were on] to one of the biggest, most terrible things in the world, but I didn't know what the hell was going on" (ibid.).

Absent personally witnessing Omarska, Gutman sought "everybody [I could find] who knew anything about what was going on in Omarska and anything about Manjaca, the one place I could go, including the Serbian government. Milosevic himself would not come to the phone, but I talked to one of his deputies" (ibid.).

Based on the two-source rule of journalism, Gutman and his editor drew up a strategy. "I went to Zagreb, where there were hundreds of thousands of Bosnian refugees," he said. "Thinking back to the World War II analogy that people do escape from concentration camps, even tightly guarded ones or they're imprisoned by mistake and they're let out, you know, by accident. Things happen, and you can find people" (ibid.).

With the help of a humanitarian organization and a week of searching, Gutman found two witnesses, one from each of two camps. "One man who said he had been in Omarska, and I think he had, he was a little bit mixed up when I talked to him. And then one guy who'd been in another camp in the town of Brcko, which is on the Sava river, and he was totally lucid, totally clear, completely convincing on everything he told me—every detail he told me, down to the names of people who had been imprisoning him and beating him and threatening him with his life," explained Gutman. "I decided that to put the story across I needed to have either two people—this is a strange formula—two people from one camp or one person from each of two camps. I needed duplication somehow, just to convince people that this was a pattern and not just a fluke. And so I found those people and then wrote that story" (ibid.).

To protect one witness's family who reportedly remained incarcerated, *Newsday* concealed his identity. "We gave him a nickname because he said he had a brother who was still in Omarska," he explained (ibid.).

For Gutman, the hard work paid off, for revealing an awful truth that otherwise may never have been known. It was "a story that was shocking, not only because of the content, but because here I am, a journalist, revealing it," he said (ibid.).

Gutman's story highlights the dogged determination driven by an ingrained sense of duty, ethic, and finely tuned emotions that signal when one's values have been violated. It's a hallmark of many—though not all—danger zone journalists who persist in the face of seemingly insurmountable obstacles and fears. With few exceptions, both local and foreign, past and present journalists interviewed for this research spoke about their duty or public service. Many expressed outrage toward the perpetrators of abuse or corruption, at the failures of those with responsibility to protect, and the pain and suffering left in their wake. That outrage, alongside compassion for victims and hope for change, propelled most interviewees to overcome obstacles, fears, and traumas.

This type of work enriched interviewed journalists' lives with a sense of purpose and relevance, according to interviews. Occasionally, their hopes that their stories would catalyze change were realized, their work rewarded by national or international action to mitigate the problems that they exposed. Too often, though, their experiences were peppered with halting disappointments, debilitating traumas, dashed hopes, and downgraded expectations. These are some of the downsides of the profession, which can discourage the once-determined journalist.

Of course, these are not the sole impetuses to a career in the "field." Travel, excitement, notoriety, and adventure were enough to draw at least one, perhaps two interviewees. Most also desired to witness history as it happened and to understand and reveal a piece of truth. And as the chapter documents, for most interviewees, it was not one or the other, but all of the above.

Duty and Outrage

"It's not some horror movie that you go to watch for fun," asserted Emmy Award-winning journalist Terry McCarthy about covering conflict. "I mean we're not there for fun, and it's certainly not fun being in a war-zone" (McCarthy 2014).

McCarthy is among the interviewed journalists who described his job as a duty, a public service, driven primarily by a desire to inform, alongside outrage at perpetrators and compassion for their victims. "If you don't have a higher goal to help others who are not there to understand it and ultimately to maybe mitigate or prevent some of the suffering, then I can't understand why anyone would do it," he said (ibid.).

McCarthy's chief goal is "to remind people there's a human cost to whatever conflict we have ... to point out that wars have enormous human costs ... If you don't believe [that], I don't know what you're doing the job for" (ibid.).

Duty called when he discovered "things that are outrageous but that people don't see in their daily lives because they're not practiced here in the United States. It's not in their face, so in a sense, it's the journalist's job to put that in their face" (ibid.).

He compared the work to discovering abuses by happenstance. "If you live next door to a house where somebody is being hurt or starved or maltreated in some way, you would find it very hard to go to bed every night hearing screams. You would intervene, either personally or you'd call the cops, or whatever," he asserted (ibid.).

Distinct from the neighbor who happens upon the offense, the foreign correspondent actively pursues the uncovering, traveling to the site of abuse to witness, document, and reveal it. "The function of a war correspondent is to extend that to locations, which are geographically far removed ... to communicate to them [that] this is happening in this country and this should stop, be it genocide in Rwanda or Darfur or violence against women," asserted McCarthy. "It's our duty to show this" (ibid.).

In this sense, McCarthy's public service is mostly geared to his home audience. "It's the media's job to be your eyes and ears. That's why we have war correspondents ... to witness a war ... We needed to show people: war is really, really bad. People die" (ibid.).

Journalists therefore provide the much-needed reality check on distortions or misinformation from war-makers and war-marketers seeking to persuade their publics to support a campaign of violence, according to McCarthy. "There is no such thing as a clinical, sanitized war. There was one defense secretary, Donald Rumsfeld, who seemed to think that you could do this—in and out, surgical strikes, and no one gets hurt, at least from our side. When America declares war, it must remember that Americans are going to die as well as whatever country they're going to," he said. "There are human costs to any war that we fought. So the next time you decide to declare war, keep that in mind" (ibid.).

They also sort fact from fictions that glorify combat: "I'm very concerned about the impression that comes across from Hollywood that we can send in these, you know, supermen, Special Forces teams with their titanium teeth, dogs, and their body armor and their radar undetectable helicopters, get the bad guys and come out without anyone being hurt. That's a completely inaccurate picture of what war is like. There are some occasions—and these Special Forces guys are very good—and there are some occasions when they do that without injury, but to think that's how you can win wars is fundamentally dishonest and misleading" (ibid.).

ABC News broadcaster Robert Woodruff concurred that disabusing audiences about the illusions of war is the danger zone journalist's primary purpose. "I think it is a way to remind people that wars are not war movies," said Woodruff. "I think people read wars and history, and all they see is the glorious moments of how the world and history was changed and the brave men and the brilliant decisions by the president and the secretary of defense. But if someone actually goes there and sees what this stuff is, and they know about the impact of it on the so-called enemies and the so-called military for your own country, you get to understand that people die; people are injured; families are impacted; people starve; entire cultures fall apart. But if you are not there to witness that, they just stay and keep reading the books and never see or really feel anything. I just think it's really important to … tell what you witnessed yourself" (Woodruff 2014).

Journalists should also counter efforts to hide the "absolute endless cover-ups," according to Woodruff. "The Patrick Tillman film is an example [because] there were no journalists there. That one remained a cover-up for such a long period of time because there was nobody there to witness it … So they really had to wait for some of the military themselves to want to tell the story, and they are under huge pressure to not to tell it" (ibid.).

The work also serves another bigger picture goal for BBC correspondent Allan Little—democratic governance. "I think at the end of the day, in a democracy, an informed population is better than an uninformed one. A democracy is stronger, a democracy is healthier if people have the truth, if people have access to even parts of the truth and if people in power are challenged. And I think that's the role. I suppose there is a kind of vocational calling about it. It's a sense of purpose and a sense of duty that guides you. It's not just about making money, earning a living. There is something, it's not about morality exactly, but there is a sense of purpose" (Little 2015).

While these goals are journalists' primary drivers, McCarthy admits that "there's an adrenaline kick that some people get, most people get— maybe." But he contends that the excitement is "not the reason you're doing it. You have to believe there's some greater reason for what you're doing, witnessing a war" (McCarthy 2014).

That "greater reason" to which McCarthy referred is grounded in a journalist's own humanity, which ostensibly distinguishes great journalism from the rest, according to Pulitzer Prize-winning journalist and professor Michael Parks: "If you lose your humanity, you're not going to function well as a reporter. At least if you're an American reporter, it's those values" (Parks 2014).

Parks's own sense of humanity and what he deemed as Western values guided many decisions when he reported from apartheid South Africa. "You know in Johannesburg, I used to do primal screams every so often because of what I had seen that day, and I had to write about it in three paragraphs" while keeping "the copy cool" (ibid.).

In one story, Parks recalled "kids stoning the house of the Anglican pastor who had run and been elected mayor in elections that were to be boycotted," he said. "I think there was a white police officer in command. But the house was being guarded by black police officers, black constables with shotguns. And a kid who was about the same age as my son stood up to throw a rock, and whether the black sergeant meant to hit him or the kid just stood up at the wrong time. [He was shot] right in the head. He was picked up, hauled away. I didn't know whether he died or not" (ibid.).

Burial records, the local medical clinic, and visits to the township all failed to identify the victim, according to Parks. But driven by his beliefs that "the dead should be named," Parks persisted, returning "when things were quieter, about two years later." But he still "couldn't find him. Went back to the township. Nobody knew of a kid about eight or nine who had been killed that day, around that day. Couldn't find him. Couldn't find him. Couldn't find him," recalled Parks. "[The] kid just disappeared. So then I started asking, 'well, why is that?' And a couple of black journalists told me the same thing: It would've been difficult for the family. [They] probably took the body back to their home village to bury [him], didn't want to be known as the family of a trouble-maker. But I came to believe that—again, values, humanity—the dead should be named. So wherever I could get the names, I put them in stories. These aren't seven nobodies. They were seven people who were killed. They were somebody's children. They were somebody's family members" (ibid.).

Parks similarly criticized reportage that favors one group of people while treating others as nameless and faceless. "Look at the way Palestinians are covered and the way Jews are covered in Israel. People slaughtered this morning [in Israel] will be named, but six people [who] died in Palestinian territories, are they named? Rarely," he said (ibid.).

Similar to Gutman, Parks strove to report institutional transgressions, particularly abuses of power by his own government. "Foreign correspondents need to hold their governments accountable. So one needs to report on that," he said. "Wars [are] being waged in the name of the American people. They need to know what's going on" (ibid.).

Parks was in Vietnam when the US "announced that they had destroyed a Viet Cong, Vietnamese communist medical facility in Cambodia, and with equipment. I thought, 'really?'" he recalled. "They destroyed medical materials. That's a clear violation of the Geneva Convention" (ibid.).

His initial source for international law was a neighbor, who was "a representative of the … International Control Commission that was set up as a consequence of the 1954 agreement that divided North and South Vietnam for a period," he explained. "And I asked him, and he said he thought that was a violation of the Geneva Convention. So I went and got a copy of the Geneva Convention at a military library [and] made notes" (ibid.).

With notes in hand and the international law in mind, Parks queried "the spokesperson for the military command in Vietnam" for a response, he said. "They were unaware that there was such a requirement in the Geneva Conventions" (ibid.).

Wars have changed since Parks reported on Vietnam, becoming murkier and more unpredictable: Frontlines are indiscernible; safe zones for journalists are hard to find. But while the wars themselves have changed, most journalists' orientations have not, according to interviews. A similar sense of duty, outrage, humanity, and compassion compels the new generation of journalists to take risks that may have been unheard of in yesterday's journalism, illustrated by the work of PC10.[1]

PC10's outrage at the wreckage and impunity, and her sympathy for victims emboldened her to report from some of the most treacherous and chaotic parts of the modern world. Braving harrowing scenarios to give victims a platform and ensure their stories did not go untold comports with her sense of duty and her emotions. "If you see all that, and you are not morally outraged … at the end of the day, if you are not somewhat touched by that or somewhat pissed off … you're just covering it as human drama that has nothing to do with you," she said. "I think it sort of reflects. I think it shows up in the work" (PC10 2014)

Through individual "human stories" that help explain broader dynamics of conflicts, their tragedies, and the triumph of the human spirit, PC10 conveyed the struggle to survive in the midst of the civil war that engulfed Syria. For example, she documented life at a "crossing that separates the government-controlled from rebel-held areas," where snipers shoot and kill people seeking to pass. But the crossing is nonetheless "packed, from people going back and forth to work, to school, to get groceries," recalled PC10. "Some of them are going just to get groceries because at that point, groceries were very expensive on the government side … People would risk [being shot] to get cheap groceries, or even just groceries they could afford, and then they would run back … They are basically running as fast as they can to try to avoid the sniper. [But] you can't really avoid a sniper, but [they try] to get through as quickly as possible, but also not too fast, [so they don't] spill the groceries that they just risked their lives for" (ibid.).

The snapshot in time fulfilled three purposes: First, it exemplified a slice of life in the throes of the Syrian civil war. Second, it revealed an essential aspect about humanity itself. "That just utterly epitomizes the human ability to overcome, that human ability to adapt ... to new circumstances ... It represents a lot of greater things." And finally, it helped explain aspects of the conflict. "There's so much [in that story] that represents the greater conflict," she said, adding, "Each story [is] just trying to get [readers] to understand just a little slice hopefully" (ibid.).

In another story, PC10 focused on "the rebel use of tunnels," which she asserted was related to "how they just know they can't face the government on the ground, so they are using [tunnels]. They dig these tunnels, and they blow them up underneath government buildings, or even non-government buildings, like buildings used by the military, which [can be] a three hundred-year-old hotel, or right by the mosque" (ibid.).

The strategy, she believes, signaled a grim reality: "They are very much willing to destroy the country in order to continue the fight, and so it's like an increasingly destructive problem on both sides. Again that just sort of tells where this conflict is now, like what happened to get us to this point," she explained (ibid.).

PC10 also witnessed and documented the despair that overcame Syria's early revolutionaries, giving way to another ominous phenomenon— child soldiers. "Before I did the child soldier story, I did one about how a lot of rebels were leaving. You know, they never signed up for a conflict for this long. Nobody thought it was going to take this long. They lost hope. They feel like what they started out with ... these calls for freedom, it really changed. So a lot of them are leaving. And then a few months later, I come back to Aleppo, and I see all these kids there on the front lines," she recalled. "All these rebels are leaving, and you know, it makes sense that now, the kids are filling up these ranks" (ibid.).

Throughout PC10's coverage of Syria, her vignettes warned about the conflict's likely trajectories. "Two years ago in Northern Syria, I was writing about when they [the rebels] started using IEDs [Improvised Explosive Devices]," recalled PC10. "They were always trying to get promises for weapons, and they weren't coming. And that was the beginning of these promises. Gulf, Arab aid or Western aid is not coming. And this was mid-2012. But they were trying to depend on themselves and started to pay for these IEDs. And even back then, I remember I put it in a story about how the Syrian conflict is already starting to resemble the Iraqi conflict and hints of that, in terms of the destruction and the indiscriminate attacks and that kind of thing" (ibid.).

Taken together, PC10's stories constructed a picture about "the desperation of the rebel opposition and just utter hopelessness of this conflict in general," she said. They simultaneously signaled a bleakness about Syria's future. "Having child soldiers is a bad thing and a bad thing for society in general because that will cause a lot of [problems] in the future" (ibid.).

These vignettes of life and death in the throes of conflict and corruption represent larger dynamics. They grab the attention of duty-bound danger zone journalists as the stories that need to be told. They are moving stories that evoke moral outrage, sympathy, or compassion, according to interviews. "Most journalists have a moral framework. They try to deny it, but they do have a very strong moral framework—and a sense of outrage. And so it wasn't exceptional that I had that in common with many other really good people," acknowledged journalist and professor John Dinges about his work in exposing human rights abuses during Chile's Pinochet dictatorship (Dinges 2014).

With his background in theology, moral outrage naturally trumped national, cultural, and political considerations for Dinges's story pursuits. "The theology, the religious background gave me, maybe a spine is one way to look at it, [and] a sense of direction," he said. "I knew where the line was all the time, morally, I mean, with principles. And that was more important to me than US policy, that sort of thing, so I didn't, I wasn't tempted to justify the US thing, which a lot of journalists did" (ibid.).

Moral outrage also supplanted personal trepidations that might have otherwise discouraged his investigations into the fates of Chileans who disappeared during Pinochet's regime. "I was [concerned], but it was not like I was running around worrying about this," said Dinges. "If something had happened to me, it was a risk I was willing to take. I don't mean to make that a big deal. It's just that I was very outraged at what was going on, and the risks that other people were taking were much, much greater than I was taking. And I had freedom of action much broader than they did, the Chilean journalists" (ibid.).

Working alongside a church-sponsored human rights organization that was "documenting everything that was happening in a very responsible, very systematic way," Dinges "[catalogued], month by month, who was disappearing and how many of them were disappearing," he said. "I often compare them [the human rights organization] to an intelligence agency because they were able to compartmentalize the information to the extent that they could confidently tell me stuff, and they knew that it wasn't going to hurt anybody because they had a system, which is what intelligence agencies do, right? They always know what they can tell you, what they can tell this person, what they can tell that person, and everybody. It's all compartmentalized. And so they were doing all this research on the organization of the secret police and what the secret police was doing … I don't even want to call it research because research is too bland a term for it" (ibid.).

Outrage propelled freelance journalist Dahr Jamail into his first foray of war correspondence, determining both his job and jobsite. With no significant prior journalism experience, Jamail "basically just dove in head first due to my own personal outrage," he said. "I saw the selling of the [Iraq] War and was completely outraged and decided, 'well, I will go in.' And one thing I can do as a US citizen is go in and report on how this is impacting the Iraqi people because that's the phase of the story that was totally omitted from the mainstream [media]" (Jamail 2014).

Knowing the subject matter for his reports, Jamail initially visited hospitals to conduct interviews with "doctors and people coming into the hospitals and [asked], 'What's going on?' 'How did you get hurt?'" (ibid.).

From there, he "started doing stories about people who were being wounded during home raids by US troops, or people who were injured from fires because there wasn't any electricity. So people were having to use oil and gas in their homes, and all kinds of accidents were happening with kids and such, and so started doing stories like that," Jamail explained (ibid.).

From those interviews, Jamail heard about "torture in Abu Ghraib and other prisons. And this was back in November 2003, so about six months before Sy [Seymour] Hersh broke that story and the photos came out" (ibid.).

He found and interviewed former Abu Ghraib prisoners "directly after they got out," he said, adding that "mainstream media didn't report on it for years later until the political climate here [in the US] shifted, allowing them to do so, but you know, that's why I was really far ahead of the curve by just literally reporting on what people were telling me on the ground and looking into this stuff" (ibid.).

After the US capture of former Iraq leader Saddam Hussein, Jamail "went out into the streets," he said, where he discovered "a school that was literally being raided by American soldiers, a secondary school for boys ... [who were] having a little, pro-Saddam demonstration, and so the military got wind of it, and detained a bunch of young school kids ... They kind of sealed it off, the military did, and then went in with pictures of the kids they wanted to detain. And then, after they got the kids and pulled out and were driving away, a bunch of kids started throwing rocks at them. And a bunch of soldiers started shooting over the heads of the kids" (ibid.).

When US forces targeted Fallujah, Jamail "reported from a clinic where they were bringing in elderly and kids who had been shot by American snipers," he said, adding that he "watched [US forces] shooting ambulances" (ibid.).

In some cases, journalists orientation comes later as a result of the events that they witness. When veteran correspondent Carol Williams began her career as a foreign correspondent, she had not intended to document the horrors and atrocities of war. Her interests were "nuclear disarmament and the superpower relationship and the quest for an end to mutual assured destruction," she said (Williams 2014).

But things changed while on an assignment covering the unraveling of Yugoslavia. Like many in her profession, the eruption of war caught Williams by surprise. "Until the Yugoslav conflict, there had not been war on the territory of Europe since World War II, and that's my life-time. And it was just unimaginable that you could see the kinds of conflicts we see today in Yugoslavia and Chechnya and Russia and Ukraine," she said (ibid.).

Her experiences there affected her coverage. "I don't pretend I went out seeking these [human rights] stories. They just happened to occur on my turf," she said. But she simultaneously "found it motivational to witness some of the most horrible things that were done to children. In Sarajevo, the Serbs would shoot into schools and hospitals. Little six-year-old kids [were] seeing their teachers blown up in front of them, ending up in hospitals with a bunch of fighters talking about how they were going to go and kill the Chetniks [and] just being ingrained with this violent outlook from very young in age" (The Scholars' Circle 2012).

Being there to witness and report the violations strengthened Williams's resolve. "Those things are difficult to see and experience, but they kept me there," she said. "The role of a journalist in that kind of circumstance is unique. And it's very empowering … There was a core of us, we're going to stay here. We don't care how damn dangerous they make it for us because the world needs to know what's going on here. And you just can't turn your back because there's not a convenient solution, to send in aid, and a UN contingent that was corrupt and basically trading on the sanctions … I never felt so relevant in my life as when I was covering the Balkans, because the world was trying to turn itself away from that conflict. It got very little press in the first couple of years. And the bad guys, the ones who were going after the most innocent and helpless targets, did this with impunity for the most part" (ibid.).

Change-Makers, Hope, and Hopelessness

"Journalism is one of the few means [that] we, maybe the only means, that I certainly had or that we have as the general public, to expose horrible practices in the hopes that somebody will do something about it. And that's what journalism's all about," argued Roy Gutman, who saw the fruits of his labor after he exposed concentration camps in Bosnia. "That story [on the camps] did have impact, and have a wallop … When I did that story, the Serbs were under the spotlight [which] to me is the best thing we can ever do as journalists, put this sort of thing under the spotlight. And they were embarrassed. And all sorts of so-called friends of Milosevic called him up and said, 'you've got to open up the place so that we can see for ourselves and let our journalists in.' And he did" (Gutman 2014).

After scores of journalists descended onto Northern Bosnia, the spotlight forced changes upon the rump Yugoslav government, according to Gutman. "You know what happened? The ethnic cleansing slowed down. It almost stopped in Northern Bosnia. The Serbs were under the spotlight. They had to use so many people just to shepherd journalists around that they had to give up on the beatings, and the torture, and the rape, and the burning of houses and the expulsions. That went on for about three months and then it resumed" (ibid.).

Gutman's hope for change fueled an unusual move for a journalist. He shared all of his sources and resources with colleagues from other, competing media. "I felt that the most important thing about my story was not that it was my story, but that the story made a difference, that it should make a difference," he said. "And you have to hope that other people, in doing their stories, will replicate yours, or at least, they might find some flaws, but that they'll come up with their own story that will expose this" (ibid.).

In the Middle East, Gutman highlighted the plights of displaced people, but this time, the international community's response was disappointing. "I tried to get the UN to react, and the US government to react, and other people to react to what I'd found, which was a very interesting exercise ... because one of the questions a reader has when he reads a story of the kind that I was doing is: 'Isn't somebody doing something about it?' And what I found by asking that question and by going for all the reactions was that the answer was 'no.' Basically, the world had abandoned these people. So it was a very strong story in that regard and a story, which to my huge regret, didn't really have much impact," he said. "I did stories in January and February [of 2014] about ISIS, just as they were starting up, because I talked to people who had been their victims. And I had really strong tales from their victims. And I was well-prepared when things developed" (ibid.).

Gutman laments that "I'm still not doing things in quite the way I would want to be doing them." But he continues nonetheless, with recalibrated goals. "I figure one of the reasons for sticking with a job, even when you have editor problems is that (a) it's a job, (b) you're in the place you want to be, (c) you can get away with a lot, and you have a platform. And you can do a lot with that platform even if it's not everything you want to do. So I'm rationalizing my way into doing a job that I feel is inadequate right now. But maybe I'll figure out some way to do it" (ibid.).

Gutman's hopes echoed those of other interviewed danger zone journalists who similarly seek to stimulate actions that alleviate suffering. Award-winning Liberian journalist Mae Azango's entire orientation is "to bring about change. I write to create a debate," she asserted. "I like to bring up these areas [subjects] so my government can address it. That's what I do ... When I write, I think about change" (Azango 2015).

Azango focuses on abuse, particularly of women and girls. "I don't like to see violence. I don't like to see people's rights being violated and most especially [against] women. So that is why I decided to report on mainly women—prostitution, rape, maternal health, human rights stories," she said (ibid.).

Through her work, Azango addressed police brutality, human trafficking and gender-based violence. "People who are doing those things and violating people have to be brought to justice," she argued. In one story, she reported on a Liberian police officer's rape of a young girl, after which he wound up in jail (ibid.).

After she exposed a sex trafficking "syndicate" that sold Liberian girls into "sex slavery in Lebanon," the Liberian government took action. "Based on that story, my government was pushed to the wall, returned 14 girls from Lebanon. That's the power of the pen" (ibid.).

Despite a taboo on the subject of female genital cutting (FGC), Azango detailed the practice and results, which affect approximately two-thirds[2] of girls. "I wanted it to become a public debate. I wanted it to become a discussion. Journalism creates debate," declared Azango. "That is why I choose the subjects, those subjects [that] will create a debate, and do something that will step on people's toes" (ibid.).

After her articles, "the government was pressured into announcing that female genital mutilation be suspended for time indefinitely," said Azango. "[It was] the first public announcement ever to be made on female genital mutilation by any government in my country" (ibid.).

The announcement was a double win for Azango and for the women who wished to be spared from the painful procedure. But the shift did not come quickly or easily. Azango's coverage of the subject landed her into trouble among the traditional communities, who threatened her and her daughter with death and torture, she said (ibid.). (Please see "Living in a Danger Zone," Chapter 5, for more on Azango's journalism.)

Still, Azango counts herself among those journalists who have enjoyed the fruits of their labor. "Nearly any story I have written I have brought about change," she said, adding that "Journalism is about making an impact ... So if you get into journalism and just write, write, write, and nothing comes out of it, I will tell you to change your profession ... That's what journalism is about. That is why the pen is mightier than the sword" (ibid.).

For award-winning Pakistani journalist, Umar Cheema, "Journalism gives me reason to live," precisely because of its power for change. "My focus is on the impact. Without impact I am doing a useless exercise. So if I am trying to change something, I want to do something that gives me [that] satisfaction. That makes the whole exercise very exciting, full of energy and full of reason ... I feel [I am] a man with a living conscience" (Cheema 2015).

Cheema targets large-scale, local offenses in the hopes of solving systemic problems. "Journalism has a great role to play in it because it grants me an opportunity; it keeps me connected with the government, people, with the problems, with the challenges, and it has given me a can-do approach," he said. "You want to tell the world what is happening, and journalism provides you that platform. When you realize that you are in a position to help people, when many people are in distress, they want somebody to help them. They want somebody to transmit their message to the authorities, and you become their source. And you know it is really satisfying, it is really exciting" (ibid.).

In 2012, Cheema read the nomination papers of all Pakistan's parliamentarians and "[cultivated] some whistle-blowers in the tax department," discovering widespread tax evasion from the very people charged with stewarding the national interest. "I took on the whole parliament, bringing to attention, unmasking the tax-evading members of parliament by showing their tax records. All the names were named, and we found out that 70 percent of them did not file their tax returns. Included among them was the president of Pakistan and half of the cabinet" (ibid.).

The findings alerted the election authorities who "double checked their taxes from the tax department and displayed everything on the website," in time for the next election (ibid.).

A follow-up report expanded the investigation's scope and prompted Pakistan's finance minister to announce "that by January 31, there will be no Member of Parliament without having a national tax number." He required they file taxes and agreed to release the "tax directory," displaying the members of parliament and the details about their paid or unpaid taxes (ibid.).

This power, Cheema said, is unique to journalism. "Unless you have your own political party and your own political brand, being just a politician, you cannot be as powerful, as assertive as a journalist. So you know, I love it." But it does not come without hazard. Cheema is one of more than 300 journalists attacked in Pakistan (Pakistani Press Foundation 2015). (His story continues in Chapter 5, "Living in a Danger Zone.")

While Pakistan ranked most dangerous country for journalists in 2014, the title was Mexico's in 2010 (International Federation of Journalists 2011; International Press Institute 2010; Portuguez and Guerrero 2011). Award-winning investigative Mexican journalist Sandra Rodriguez Nieto was there, reporting on the descent of Ciudad Juarez into a dark abyss in which cartels and soldiers determined who lived and who died. "These people are suffering," said Rodriguez Nieto (2014) about the residents of Ciudad Juarez, which at the time was called the "murder capital of the world" (Valencia 2015). But Rodriguez Nieto was not content with reporting yet another "anecdote for some crime," she said, and instead sought to reveal the "bigger forces" behind the suffering, to solve the problems at their roots. "I think I became a journalist because I wanted to change the world, as many others [do]" (Rodriguez Nieto 2014).

With the methodology of a skilled detective, Rodriguez Nieto compiled data sets, analyzed patterns, and pieced together a surprising set of factors that ostensibly fueled the rampant corruption, lethal violence, and impunity. Each symptom intertwined with broader forces, including the global economy, the legal system, even local geography. In Juarez, "you can see the effects of global policies in human life" (ibid.) (detailed further in Chapter 5, "Living in a Danger Zone").

However, with problems so entrenched, Rodriguez Nieto's hopes for change were dashed. "I don't feel the same now, I have to say," she admitted. Years of analysis and reporting, yet "nothing has changed," she said. "I believe journalism has this power, but it's not going beyond public exposure. Nothing has been solved … How could I keep on working and not get totally disappointed?" (ibid.)

Frustrated and disillusioned, Rodriguez Nieto downgraded her "big expectations," settling instead for "keeping the record," she said. "Now I think that even if we don't change the world, if we don't see the change, we have to keep on being committed to tell the story because the story is very important … Now I work despite the fact that I don't see any change. I work because it's my duty. And I think that's very important … [It is] a lot of work, and that's our duty as journalists. And if we do it properly, I think it's better" (ibid.).

Rodriguez Nieto is not alone in downgrading her hopes and goals for her journalism. PC10 and the BBC's Allan Little both settled for important but less ambitious goals through their journalism—establishing and correcting the historical record, in the face of silence, misinformation, or propaganda—a sometimes Herculean task in itself.

PC10's frustrations mounted as the international powers turned away from the crises in Syria. Despite her in-depth coverage, Syria's conditions deteriorated beyond her imagination. "The whole thing is very, very frustrating," she said. "I am writing about Nusra and the Al Qaeda movement, [and] they're starting to act like ISIS. And it's like a new ISIS. And it is just a horrible situation that keeps getting worse and worse. At every point we feel like, 'no, no, no, we've definitely gotten to the worst.' Then something else [worse] comes. So now you have rebels who are so fractured, and you have ISIS, and now you have Nusra. Then you have the regime, and then you have civilians who are completely caught in between … the bombing, the barrel bombs all over Syria, and then just with the constant artillery. And nobody cares about that anymore. The talk is purely about ISIS, even though what ISIS does is really nothing compared to what the regime has done. And it's a very convenient way for us to like pivot focus" (PC10 2014).

Her colleagues express similar confusion over the inaction. "They don't understand how we've shown all this stuff that's happened, and nobody has done anything," she said. "I have friends who covered conflicts in Africa and felt the same way, even maybe more so in Africa. In Syria, at least it gets sort of attention [whereas] in Africa, sometimes those conflicts just don't even get attention … You could write about some of the most brutal things that are happening, and nobody cares. We still have these journalists who are risking their lives and putting themselves in such danger to get out a story that has no impact. They were just as confounded that not more has been done" (ibid.).

Like Gutman and Rodriguez Nieto, PC10 lowered her expectations when hope for change had been dashed. "In terms of most conflicts, you know, we've been covering it for years and nothing has really happened," she said. "It doesn't feel like our coverage has had much effect one way or the other. I mean, I think it's still important, for sure. But yeah I think any hope of it affecting policy is long gone" (ibid.).

Now, she primarily seeks to witness and record pieces of truth from complicated conflicts. "There has to be a drive in terms of that need to bear witness, that need to document," acknowledged PC10, adding, "Libya, Egypt, Syria, it's all very, very confusing, [and] the actors are not thinking about how can I make this easy for the journalist. They are in very confusing conflicts" (ibid.).

For Little, it was Bosnia that "was profoundly disillusioning," he said. "To me and to almost everybody who was involved covering that story on the ground, there was a clear injustice. It was one massive injustice at the heart of that war. And the policies that the Western democracies adopted towards the war didn't recognize it. The policies of the Western democracies were that all sides were equally guilty, and this was manifestly not true. And I got more and more disillusioned by that. It didn't matter how much reporting there was, how much eye-witness engagement was actually going on, it was still British and French, less so American, but the British and French governments kept standing up and saying, 'well, of course, they're all as bad as each [other]'" (Little 2015).

These responses struck Little as violations of "one of the key tenets of post-1945 security arrangements, which was that there would be collective action to defend the weak against the strong. And it wasn't happening. And then there was ethnic cleansing. Absolutely clear. They all knew it was happening. Everybody knew it was happening. Srebrenica was absolutely predictable. We all predicted it. We all knew it was going to happen. I wrote a piece in 1993, which was never broadcast, saying, 'When Srebrenica falls, whether it's next week or next month or next year, and hundreds of men are taken into a field and shot, and buried in mass graves—when that happens, let none of say we didn't know, because we do know.' And it wasn't broadcast. My editor back in London thought it was intemperate and partisan" (ibid.).

Little recognized a long line of journalists who experienced similar disillusionments and reiterated the words of late correspondent Martha Gellhorn, who famously said: "I thought all I had to do toward injustice, to right it, was to reveal it. And I think I must have thought of public opinion as some kind of solid force, something like a tornado, always ready to blow on the side of the angels, which of course you eventually become disillusioned about. You know that no matter how much revealing you do, public opinion is very often completely unmoved. It doesn't want to blow on the side of the angels" (ibid.).

Like Gellhorn and many of her successors, Little concluded that "keeping the record straight, sorting out myth from reality, sorting out propaganda from truth is in itself a form of honorable behavior involving reader and writer, a form of honorable behavior in which reader and writer take part together, and that's good enough for me" (ibid.).

During the Iraq War, for example, Little and his colleague physically counted the dead to settle a dispute between the Iraqi government and the Allied Powers, which had both exaggerated the death toll, the former to accuse the latter, and the latter to deflect criticism. The one-by-one count set the record straight about the true number of human casualties (ibid.) (detailed more in Chapter 6, "The First Casualty").

Both Vice News' Danny Gold and New Zealand freelance journalist Jon Stephenson had long abandoned hope for change through journalism. For Stephenson, establishing the historical record is key. "[I] don't have any illusions about the impact of our work. [I] don't think that we're going to write something and everyone's going to go, 'Holy crap! That's really bad, I'm going to change my view ... and we're going to seriously pressure our government to do A, B, C,'" he said. "My view is that by documenting it as carefully as possible and putting it out there, and challenging that narrative ... It'll be there in at least one form or another. It'll be part of history. It'll be on the record" (Stephenson 2014).

Unsettled by the post-9/11 Western powers' narrative, Stephenson ventured unilaterally into Afghanistan to understand a host of looming questions including the country's history, the motivations of the attackers, and the coming foreign policy responses to the 9/11 attacks. "We were getting all this sort of propaganda, and a lot of very simplistic reporting ... from the US administration ... repeated through the media about terrorism and terrorists and evildoers and so on," he said. "Nobody really understood ... about Afghanistan. It was really a case of going and having a look" (ibid.).

The resulting policies, he believed, would be "pretty extensive" and important to record as an eye-witness. "What makes someone want to endure this sort of punishment?" he asked, referring to the reprisals from the United States and its allies. "I mean, really, what they were going through was hell ... I think there were about 600 to 900 of them up in the mountains. Apparently some of them had wives and kids with them as well, so you know it really made you think ... what is going on here that people are prepared to do this, or endure this day after day, because it went on for a fortnight ... That made me sort of think, 'Wow, these guys must really hate America, or really hate the West, and what are the roots of that hatred?'" (ibid.).

But Stephenson's primary focus remained on his own country's involvement, which he believed had not been truthfully reported. "That's been a big weakness with New Zealand's coverage of the so-called war on terror because we haven't had [witnesses] in Afghanistan ... talking to the people we're working with or trying to investigate what is happening to prisoners that we've been involved with, or going to the villages which we've raided. You can find out a lot by going on the ground that you can never find out back [reporting from home]. Of course, that's very difficult work" (ibid.).

Questions such as these made it important to physically go to Afghanistan and "get the detail," said Stephenson, adding that he has "never been fascinated going from war to war. I don't think like that ... There are some people, there are a lot of correspondents that just want to go from one conflict to another, actually focused on being in the field. Reporting on conflict on the ground, but to me, and to me that's a very important role, but I think what I've come to realize is just how limited that can be" (ibid.).

In the end, Stephenson found that many of those questions remained unanswered. "I probably left Afghanistan with a lot more questions than answers" (ibid.).

With a "faint hope that maybe something will happen," Gold advises against harboring hope for change. "If you go in thinking your report is going to change something, you're going to drive yourself crazy," he warned. "99% of the time it's not going to make a difference. So you look at, how long was Nicholas Kristof writing about Darfur for? In the biggest publication, biggest audience ever. Did it make much of a difference? ... Some of these problems really don't have an easy solution or a solution at all" (Gold 2014).

Gold chides journalists who give false hope to sources. "People talk to you sometimes, they have these expectations that if you talk to them, it's going to change things, and you have to be clear with them that it's not. I hate it when journalists say, 'Just tell us your story. You'll see this, and people need to know.' Don't patronize people. Don't give people hope that something's going to change ... Most people in the world don't care about the suffering and problems of other people" (ibid.).

Questions at Home

Sometimes danger zone stories originate in the minds of foreign correspondents, from the questions they believe they should be asking on behalf of their audiences at home, according to Parks: "What was happening in the war to their sons and daughters? What was happening to the war as a national effort? Was it going to succeed? Was it going to fail? Did it succeed? Did it accomplish what was intended? Did it accomplish things that weren't intended?" (Parks 2014).

Bob Woodruff sought answers to "the biggest" questions, such as "the ones that impact our country the most. I think that's without question. And that's true with news generally. So I think obviously the wars that involve the US-service members, armies and navies and things are the most important. The other ones, of course, would be conflicts involved that ... affect our economy. That could be any conflicts within Asia that would affect China, which then of course affects the economy of the United States. Sadly, I think the ones that [do not affect] economic zones that are important to the United States, then it's probably less likely you're going to cover those conflicts. So Africa has very few conflicts that are covered, as much as conflicts that would be in [say] Ukraine and Russia, because Russia is a huge part of the world economy and is right next to Europe," explained Woodruff (Woodruff 2014).

The wars raging in the Middle East ranked high: "Iraq and Afghanistan, those are wars that completely changed the coverage of wars, and completely changed the attitudes about our relationships towards the Middle East generally," he said, suggesting that he sought to understand "just what we need to do to try to improve our relationship with the Middle East." (Ibid.).

Woodruff simultaneously lamented the paucity of "knowledge about the thousands of years of conflicts that would have an impact on how successful those invasions would be. There was so little known about Sunnis and Shiites amongst the people … with their feet on the ground in the sands of the Middle East, [who] didn't understand that it wasn't going to be this simple [task] to bring peace to a part of the world where peace never was" (ibid.).

In contrast, Gold prefers reporting on under-covered parts of the world. "I do a lot of stories that people don't focus on, like Burma. People have reported on Burma, but it doesn't get a lot of attention especially in America," he said. For stories that have received more attention, Gold seeks new angles. "I don't think I do stories people haven't already covered. I just do it in a different way or focus on a different issue" (Gold 2014).

For one story, Gold heard a tip about Trinidad that piqued his interest. "I lived in a Trinidadian neighborhood, and I'd be on the corner with like my neighbors, and we'd all drink Coronas together," he said. "And they said, 'You should do a story on Trinidad' … And I started looking into it, and I thought, 'you know what, this is a great story.'" The "great story" became a documentary series exploring life-and-death issues facing the country (ibid.).

Historically, some newspapers were more indulgent about less popular issues, according to Parks, who spent "a summer doing wars you never heard of" while working for *The Baltimore Sun*. His editor trusted reporters "to come up with their own stories … I was based in Cairo, and there [were] a bunch of little wars, Libya and Togo, [each] had a border war. Who knew? But people died. Spain and Morocco were at war in the Sahara. Who knew? But people died" (Parks 2014).

The Sources

Formal and informal sources, some met by chance and some purposefully developed while at the job, provide informational tidbits, the bases of stories. Parks cultivated sources and relationships by "visiting people" or "sipping tea," usually without "having a particular story in mind." Through conversations, he "heard things," little bits of information that culminated in bigger stories. Other interviewees knew what they wanted to know and sought sources who might provide that information (ibid.).

Foreign correspondents rely upon their local guides, or "fixers," a catchall term for their local hires who translate, advise, drive, secure official visas, to help find the most important stories. With in-depth local knowledge, the guides are often at the heart of the foreign correspondents' stories. Freelance journalist Balint Szlanko relied on his Ukrainian fixer "for a lot of news. He was very well-plugged into what was going on, and he was great, sort of well-aware, and he was great at figuring out what was going on and what to do and what not to do. You need a local guide. There's no other way. Even if you speak the language, you still need a local guide most of the time" (Szlanko 2014).

Journalists also rely on each other for stories, often discussing the developments of the day. Szlanko recalled, for example, getting tips from colleagues and colleagues of colleagues. One photographer from St. Petersburg for example, "was friends with the Reuters photographer, who was also from Russia. And they talked every day [asking], 'What's going on? What's going on?' Helping each other" (ibid.).

That's how Szlanko discovered some of his "color pieces," such as the Ukrainian rebel commander's wedding, which provided a juxtaposition of contradictory images: "There were all these rebels dressed in kind of flowers, and they had their bouquets of flowers in their hands, sort of waiting for the boss to turn up. And then the boss turned up, and he was wounded, and he had his arm in a cast. And then the bride turns up and the bride is, she's a foot taller than the bridegroom. It all looks hilarious, frankly. And they all go in and there [are] snipers in the building, protecting the building in case somebody wants to assassinate the boss. And everybody at the wedding is either a rebel soldier or a journalist. And the register is conducting the thing in the name of the Donetsk Peoples' Republic, which is a state nobody recognizes, raising the interesting question as to whether the wedding is even legal ... It was something out of a film, frankly. So we did that, and people loved it. People in the office back in London were all [rejoicing]. 'This is great. We were getting bored of the shelling anyway. Can you do more stories like this?'" (ibid.)

The story exchange often occurs informally, according to McCarthy. "Why all journalists drink together is because they all have interesting stories to tell ... And, often, just in the course of a lunch or a dinner, you will get a couple of story ideas," he said. But he adds, "Journalists are not that imaginative. A lot of it comes from what's been in the press already" (McCarthy 2014).

The Personal is Professional

Professional interests culminate from personal experiences, evoking empathy that provides news stories. Journalists from Northern Ireland who had lived through the "troubles," for example, experienced trauma, sorrow, frustration, or anguish from the oppression and violence that they personally experienced, which motivated their coverage (discussed in "Living in a Danger Zone," Chapter 5). Liberian journalist, Mae Azango's stories also focused on people who suffered similar abuses that she had faced in her life (discussed more in "Living in a Danger Zone," Chapter 5). And PJ09's[3] immigration struggles fueled her desire to shed light onto others' migration pains. "You leave your country, your family, your job. Then you're in a new country," she said of her own experience. "Nobody knows who you are, and plus the language was a huge issue ... I was just terrified" (PJ09 2014).

Those interests took her to the border of Mexico and the US where she walked and interviewed migrants, documenting their stories, writing profiles and reporting the very "harsh situations that you face as an immigrant," she said. "I actually walked the whole three-plus thousand miles ... It was just my backpack and my camera" (ibid.).

But PJ09's findings turned out much grimmer than she imagined— cartel-controlled territories, a human slave trade, rife with human rights abuses and murders. "[Traffickers] were abducting people—women [and] transfer[ring them] like merchandise," she said, adding, "Everybody says human trafficking is sexual, but it's ... more than that. It's a slavery workforce" (ibid.).

PJ09 met single mothers who were forced to work "for those networks for pennies ... Some of them do it for shelter and food," with ten or more unknown men in their homes, she explained. "They were terrified ... They just received pennies ... People who work for the traffickers, there's another side of the story" (ibid.).

Both men and women fell victim to the cartels, and bemoaned their circumstances to PJ09, "You have to work with them. You have to pay them to let you do your job" (ibid.).

The tragedies seemed never ending—"case after case of sexual violations, people dying, threats, killing" and abductions for purposes of blackmail and extortion. "There was a guy who escaped from the kidnapping [who told me that the traffickers] got around 20 people," said PJ09. "It was here in Tijuana, Tecate area, and they took them to a kind of hill, like a mountain, and they start calling [their] people, asking for money, the family of those immigrants. And [if] they say they don't have money to pay, they kill [the migrants]. This guy told me that he saw those traffickers kill six, seven people. And he found a way to escape" (ibid.).

At first, the stories were unfathomable for PJ09 and for her editor. "It was too cruel to believe. It was so unbelievable ... that the traffickers, the narco-traffickers were killing these immigrants like that" (ibid.).

Yet the witnesses went "on record, on video. We went to the area with this guy. We protect[ed] his identity of course," said PJ09. And he took an additional step: "He presented the case to the human rights department of Mexico. Even for them it was, 'We need to confirm this is really happening.' But yeah, they confirmed it."

Evidence continued to mount, and the witness's predictions came to fruition. "He told me [that] the bodies are going to start to show ... by December," She recalled. "Why December? He said, 'Because most of the people, they cross the border in November, December. It's a busy, busy time because of the weather. It's not as hot. And because for the traffickers ... it's the time [for] picking the 'harvest' ... It was a couple of months later ... I had this unbelievable story about 11 people in Tijuana, and then they found a house with 72 bodies" (ibid.).

Personal influences are not always born of suffering. Journalists "have their private agendas. Everyone is driven by their own personal history and their own demons in some cases," according to McCarthy (2014). In some cases, long-enduring political or historic interests are the journalist's muse, drawing them deeper into their subjects. Freelance journalist Balint Szlanko, for example, was "always interested in the Middle East, so I started doing, started working on [stories], doing trips to the Middle East on a freelance basis," he said. "And I set out to be a general kind of Middle East guy, and I just got drawn into these war stories" (Szlanko 2014).

As a self-identified "history buff," Szlanko was "fascinated" with strategic aspects of the Middle East, which he called "a realist's paradise in foreign policy terms [with] a lot of stuff going on. It's very complicated ... When I started covering Afghanistan in 2008, I was interested in the army, what the army was doing," he said. "It wasn't a conventional war. It was what you call a counter-insurgency" (ibid.).

Immersed in the region and observing its changes, Szlanko grew interested in development issues and their uses in conflict. "One of the aspects of counter-insurgency is state-building. You're trying to strengthen the state that you're supporting. In that case the west was trying to build the Afghan state to the point where it could look after itself. So I became interested in developmental issues there," he explained, adding, "I'm really interested in the strategy aspects of war, like why states and groups within states fight" (ibid.).

As the Middle East became embroiled in more upheavals and conflict, his reporting followed suit. "If you cover the Middle East these days, that means covering conflict, really because that's what it is, particularly since 2011," he said. "I just kind of got caught up in it. And now I'm really only doing wars" (ibid.).

More recently, Szlanko's interest in human rights has grown, though he admits, "I wasn't [so interested] in the beginning, to be perfectly honest" (ibid.).

Passions range broadly among danger zone journalists. "Some people are interested in strategy. I met people who are interested in weapons. I know one guy who's into guns. That's his thing," said Szanko. Others are drawn to the excitement of travel, the craft itself, the feelings of relevance, and the front seat to history being made. "There is the excitement, certainly. It is an exciting job. I won't deny that. Most of my colleagues, I think, all of my colleagues would concur [that] it's an exciting job. You get to travel. There is the pressure and all that," said Szlanko. "And I like writing, although [now] … I'm in television. I've become interested in television itself. I enjoy editing now. I enjoy seeing my stories on TV. All these things. I enjoy the freedom of it. I come and go, plan new trips. I'm not stuck in an office. All these things matter" (ibid.).

Gold agreed. "People try to pretend, 'I don't do it for the adrenaline.' And I'm sure that's not the main reason, but it's definitely something that makes them want to keep doing it," he said. And amid harrowing or difficult experiences, the job is "kind of fun sometimes. It's exciting. There are moments that are really tough stuff, but you do some crazy, crazy things. You go to places where you're not supposed to be, like nowhere you should ever go," explained Gold. "You end up in places where you have no business being. It's exciting sometimes. Yeah, it's fun. Moments are fun. Yeah, you get some pretty amazing moments" (Gold 2014).

For these reasons, journalists who have left the "field" for executive jobs do miss the more exciting part of the job (Mojica 2014).

Stories are sometimes born of the basic need to make a living. For instance, Szlanko originally covered the Ukrainian conflict "for business reasons, really," he said. "I never really wanted to do Ukraine. But I'm based out of Budapest in Hungary, and it's on my doorstep, I suppose. I got pulled into that. I was offered assignments by various people, and I couldn't really turn them down" (Szlanko 2014).

News norms, not personal interests, dictate these types of stories. "If you're in a war at the height of the war, then the stories will, it's going to be fighting, basically—fighting, hospitals, refugees, civilian hardship, rubble, that kind of thing. And the news cycle dictates a lot of it. So for example, if you work for a news agency, and there's ongoing fighting, then the demand from the office will be, 'What's happened today?' There was shelling somewhere, five civilians were killed. Okay, that's a story. You go there; you film it," said Szlanko. "When I was in Ukraine in July we were doing sort of daily reporting, so every day, shelling, shelling, shelling, hospitals, refugees, that kind of thing" (ibid.).

Despite Szlanko's initial disinterest in covering the conflict in Ukraine, he acknowledged the excitement of documenting history as it was being made. "The war in Ukraine right now, this is the first war in Europe for 20 years, 15 years, I suppose. It seems to herald a new era of great power competition if you like, between the West and Russia. Again that's history in the making, and it's interesting for me to be there and to see how it plays out" (ibid.).

Opportunities to advance a career or make a name for oneself have also ostensibly attracted danger zone journalists, say interviewees. Szlanko refers to some of these reasons as the "baser" ones for pursuing the field. "They thought it was a kind of dashing thing to do" (ibid.).

But other interviewees, such as Gutman, find these reasons to be "really madness." He criticized one correspondent who found himself kidnapped in Syria, ostensibly "for adventure, and also so that he could write a book and sell it" (Gutman 2014).

Stephenson also denounced correspondents who were "feeding the beast," in the "theater of journalism ... There are a lot of people in front of a portable satellite camera saying, 'Well Bill, here we are at the frontline, and the Americans are bombing very heavily, and you can see behind me, the mountains where the Al Qaeda forces are blah, blah, blah ... and there are rumors that bin Laden is there, and you know today the bombing seemed to intensify,'" he recalled. "They knew very little about apart from [that] there's fighting, and we want to capture the 'bang bang' ... That was about it. There's no context. There was very little interest in what the locals had to say ... There was very little emphasis on the human cost of the war in terms of the wrong people being bombed, perhaps, [and] there was very little insight. It was almost jingoistic" (Stephenson 2014).

In Stephenson's estimation, the claim that these journalists are driven by a sense of morality or public interest was "absolute bullshit," he said. "I am sure they were after good stories and interesting news, but I think it was a whole lot of people struggling to come to terms with a complex topic that they knew very little about apart from [that] there is fighting" (ibid.).

But these impetuses are not the norm, according to McCarthy, who said, "Almost everyone that I worked with has some sense that they have a duty to report and expose what they see ... Some correspondents took inordinate risks or exposed themselves more than others would. And the reasons they might've done that are multifarious and could be rooted in their own personal histories" (McCarthy 2014).

Notes

1 PC10 asked not to be identified for reasons of safety.
2 UNICEF http://www.childinfo.org/files/FGCM_Lo_res.pdf.
3 PJ09 asked to have their identity concealed.

References

Azango, Mae. 2015. Personal Interview. Via Telephone from Auckland. September 2.
Cheema, Umar. 2015. Personal Interview. Via Skype. Auckland to Islamabad. August 17.
Dinges, John. 2014. Personal Interview. In Person. Washington, DC. November 3.
Gold, Danny. 2014. Personal Interview. In Person. Brooklyn, NY. October 31.
Gutman, Roy. 2014. Personal Interview. Via Skype. Auckland to Istanbul. December 6.

International Federation of Journalists. 2011. "IFJ Reports 97 Journalists Were Lost to Violence in 2010." http://www.ifex.org/international/2011/01/04/journa lists_killed_2010/. Accessed March 26, 2016.

International Press Institute. 2010. "Mexico Most Dangerous Country for Journalists, IPI Says." *Latin American Herald Tribune.* http://laht.com/article.asp? ArticleId=366139&CategoryId=14091. Accessed March 26, 2016.

Jamail, Dahr. 2014. Personal Interview. Via Telephone. November 10.

Little, Allan. 2015. Personal Interview. Via Telephone. Auckland to London. January 27.

McCarthy, Terry. 2014. Personal Interview. In Person. Los Angeles. July 7.

Mojica, Jason. 2014. Personal Interview. In Person. Brooklyn, NY. October 31.

Pakistani Press Foundation. 2015. "No Country for Journalists." November 26. http://www.pakistanpressfoundation.org/2015/11/no-country-for-journalists/. Accessed March 26, 2016.

Parks, Michael. 2014. Personal Interview. Los Angeles. November 18.

PC10. 2014. Personal Interview. In Person. Site withheld. November 11.

PJ09. 2014. Personal Interview. In Person. Site withheld. November 10.

Portuguez, Enid and Mariela Hoyer Guerrero. 2011. "Renowned Journalist and Family Killed in Mexico." International Press Institute. http://ipi.freemedia.at/ newssview/article/renowned-journalist-and-family-killed-in-mexico.html. Accessed March 26, 2016.

Rodriguez Nieto, Sandra. 2014. Personal Interview. Via Skype. Los Angeles to Mexico City. November 17.

Stephenson, Jon. 2014. Personal Interview. In Person. Auckland, NZ. December 12.

Szlanko, Balint. 2014. Personal Interview. Via Skype. November 12.

The Scholars' Circle. 2012. "Reporting from the Danger Zone." Panel Discussion. First broadcast September 30.

Valencia, Nick. 2015. "After Years of Violence and Death, 'Life is Back' in Juarez." CNN. April 21. http://www.cnn.com/2015/04/21/americas/mexico-ciuda d-juarez-tourism/.

Williams, Carol. 2014. Personal Interview. In Person. Los Angeles. June 26.

Woodruff, Bob. 2014. Personal Interview. Via Telephone. Los Angeles to New York. November 13.

3   The Foreign Correspondent's Afflictions

Abducted in Syria

The events unfolded remarkably like other journalist abductions. A screaming masked gunman thrust an AK-47 into the face of the journalists' driver. Within seconds, the gunman and his dozen or so cohort dragged the three journalists—Hungarian reporter, Balint Szlanko, Mexican reporter, Temoris Grecko, and Basque photographer, Andoni Lubaki—from the car. They blindfolded and handcuffed the three media men, confiscated their belongings, including Grecko's glasses, and tossed the men into a prison cell (Szlanko 2013).

Theirs was a shorter detention than those of some other abducted journalists, such as David Rohde or Jill Carol, who remained imprisoned for eight and three months, respectively. But the experience was terrifying, nonetheless, leaving Szlanko with a diminished "sense of security," he said (Szlanko 2014).

These ordeals can impair journalists' personal and professional lives, heightening insecurity, diminishing enthusiasm for their passion or what many correspondents perceive as their duty, ultimately affecting their reportage. "It's damaging," said Szlanko. "It corrodes your sense of security ... This whole kidnapping thing; that's made me paranoid. It's made me rethink my whole modus operandi in these areas" (ibid.).

Prior to the abduction, Szlanko had moved comfortably around the Middle East. But after the incident and repeated deployments to conflict zones, particularly Ukraine, the realities of war and its dangers really sunk in. "I felt I just couldn't deal with the shelling anymore. I was getting scared basically, because the big booms, and the knowledge of what that does to people and everyday seeing the rubble and seeing the injured and seeing the dead. I was like, 'I don't want to be here anymore because it's just too scary,'" he said. "In the beginning, that was fine because you deal with it, [but] for me it was getting progressively harder and harder" (ibid.).

After three weeks of reporting from the Ukraine conflict, war-weariness set in, and Szlanko found himself "counting the days" until he could leave. "The war there turned into conventional mechanized war, which essentially means a lot of artillery shelling," he recalled. "I went down there for a week, and I got extended for two weeks. Then I got extended for another one. I was there for three weeks, and they asked me, 'Do you want to stay for another week?' And by then … I felt I just couldn't deal with it" (ibid.).

When asked to work another week in Ukraine, Szlanko declined. "I reached the end of my tether after three weeks," he said. "I didn't want to stay there anymore … I wanted to go home because this doesn't feel safe anymore … I feel that my sense of security has been damaged, not considerably, but enough that I'm aware of it, because I've been doing this every month or every other month for the past five years" (ibid.).

Although Szlanko doesn't believe he has Post-Traumatic Stress Disorder (PTSD), he admits that his tolerance has diminished. "If you're going to ask me point blank, 'do you have nightmares?' No, I don't," he said. But he added, "It bothers me in the sense that it pains me. It hurts me to see … Some of it is quite stressful" (ibid.).

Szlanko muses that if he were to change jobs, he would "never go back to a war-zone again," he said. "I would probably get back to my normal phase again. I would be fine" (ibid.).

Abducted in Congo

Vice News journalist and producer Andrew Glazer endured a frightful two-day ordeal in Congo that took him months to process and diminished his desire to cover dangerous regions, particularly Congo. "It was the end of our trip in Congo," he said. "We were kidnapped on our way to the airline. We were walking to change our tickets … when we were arrested" (Glazer 2014).

Held at gunpoint for some six hours, Glazer and his colleagues endured intense interrogation. "It felt just like a movie," he said, admitting that he initially found it humorous and believed "the guys were eventually going to let us go, [so] that didn't feel as scary." But the following day's events terrified them. Gunmen abducted the two journalists, "picked us up … [and] knocked [us] around" (ibid.).

The gunmen forced Glazer and his colleague into a car, and the driver raced away. With no information about the abductors, their motivations, or to where they were being driven, Glazer feared for his life. "I started imagining what was going to happen to us, because we had obviously pissed people off" (ibid.).

Distressed by their expected fate, the journalists decided to try for an escape. As the car sped down the street, Glazer and his colleague forced open the door and leapt out. "We actually jumped from a moving car and ran into a crowd. That was a scary time" (ibid.).

In retrospect, Glazer believed the two incidents were related but admits, "I don't really know, so that was unsettling as well. It could've been completely random. We still to this day don't know" (ibid.).

The experience was deeply disturbing, causing nightmares and a profoundly impaired sense of security, that "made me reticent to go back to Congo," he said. "I never thought I wanted to go back to Congo, until a week ago" (ibid.).

Abducted in Bosnia

On a seemingly "quiet day" in Bosnia, BBC correspondent Allan Little and his colleagues spotted what he described as "a column of hundreds of foreign fighters ... with green bandanas and flags" who "clearly weren't Bosnian" (Little 2015). Their interest piqued, Little and his crew assembled to film them—"A mistake," he acknowledged. "We were instantly seized with pistols at our heads and marched into their headquarters ... They were so hostile to us" (ibid.).

Convinced that the BBC production team were spies, the self-named Afghan Arab Corps set up a makeshift court where they would try the journalists for espionage. If found guilty, the punishment would be death. "It was terrifying because it was made clear to us that the penalty for spying was to be shot, and that justice would be instant" (ibid.).

The tribunal consisted of "three men sitting there at a desk, the judges" who called up "evidence," which included "a so-called television expert to examine our cameras." The "expert" testified that the BBC camera was "the sort of camera issued by Mossad, and so we were 'Israeli spies,' and the camera was 'deadly ... sending evidence back live to the enemy in the next town.' We were [allegedly] 'betraying their position and their numbers'" (ibid.).

The "judges" called up additional "witnesses" who all testified that, "'Yes, I saw the spies running away'" (ibid.).

That's when the Bosnian law enforcement officers arrived, resulting in a "stand-off" between the two groups. Little and the crew were "handed over" to the police, rescuing the BBC crew from what seemed an inevitable fate (ibid.).

Local police, now in charge of "keeping an eye on the foreigners that fell into the hands of the Afghan Arabs," told Little and his colleagues, "Okay, I'll do my best here. But you're in big shit. You should not have come to town today. These foreign Muslims are out of control. And my life is in danger from them as well because I'm the inspector for foreigners. They don't trust me. I'm not even a Muslim, I'm a Croat. And that woman who's gone out with your colleague to get the passport, she's been put in my office to spy on me. And so when she comes back, we didn't have this conversation. Okay?" But "the local police knew that it would be disastrous for them if four western journalists were murdered in a town that was undisputedly under the control of the Bosnian government, not accidently killed or caught in crossfire on the frontline, but murdered in a town where there were no Serbs" (ibid.).

Their relief was temporary. When his colleague returned from retrieving his passport, he "was as white as a ghost, and we said, 'What's wrong with you? And he said, 'The building's surrounded by Muj, and they want the foreigners back'" (ibid.).

Negotiations "lasted ages and ages," said Little. "There was a long, long exchange … between the police chief in the next room and the Muj commander outside on walkie-talkies, where the Muj commander said, 'We want the spies back.' And the police chief was telling them, 'Stay away.' We thought the building was going to be stormed, and we would be seized. So it was all pretty tense, as you can imagine" (ibid.).

In the end, "the local police got their way and rescued us," said Little. "The Muj backed down. And I've no idea why they backed down, but they did … It was pretty terrifying" (ibid.).

The Returns

Unlike local journalists, soldiers, and residents of danger zones, foreign correspondents usually deploy to the hotspots for shorter durations and with greater freedom to leave, which helps prevent long-lasting psychological injury, according to interviews. "You don't have these long tours. The army is doing, in Iraq, 12, sometimes 15 month tours. And most journalists don't do 15 month assignments," said veteran journalist Terry McCarthy (2014).

ABC newsman Bob Woodruff, who endured a brain injury while reporting from Iraq, agreed, asserting that his trauma was "purely physical … because I had not been over there on a long deployment. It wasn't a year and a half or something. That's what creates a lot of PTS" (Woodruff 2014).

Repeated deployments, however, can be as hazardous as long-term assignments, according to interviewees. It's the bane of the tried-and-true danger zone correspondent who is regularly tapped to move from one danger zone to another. "Once you've done a few wars, your bosses think, 'Oh, he or she gets it. So next crisis, put her on the plane and fly her in.' And so you accumulate over the years a bunch of wars, and yet you're meant to be indestructible because you're not being shot at. You're not a soldier, so you can just check out of your hotel and fly to the next war," explained McCarthy (The Scholars' Circle 2012).

But the assumptions of media managers fail, as trauma compounds. After a series of assignments in "intense periods" covering conflicts in Sri Lanka and Cambodia and later in Afghanistan and Iraq, McCarthy experienced the toll. "[I was] pretty frazzled. [I] didn't like to hear cars backfire, and really needed to chill out. These things, they seem to mount up, and you reach a point where you really need to just get away from it," he said (McCarthy 2014).

Over time, the career success becomes inversely proportional to the correspondent's well-being, according to Vice News' Danny Gold. "Stuff builds over time ... The better you get at it, the more work you do, the less happy you are as a person. The more successful you are, the less happy you're going to be because you're going to see more shit" (Gold 2014).

To cope with the stress, interviewees attempt to stagger their assignments and down time, according to Szlanko. "I found that some of that stays with you if you keep doing the job," he said. "If you go home, okay, and you're on a holiday for a couple of weeks, you rest, and you can go back again. But if you keep going back and back and back, I think there may be at least some semi-permanent damage" (Szlanko 2014).

Second-Hand Trauma

Personal trauma to self is one hazard of danger zone journalism. But experiencing others' tragedies, losses, and anguish also traumatizes correspondents, including many interviewed for this research. Freelance journalist Dahr Jamail, who endured three close calls during the Iraq War, argued that "You can get just as much trauma secondarily by interviewing people, like torture survivors, or people who have had family members killed" (Jamail 2014).

Jamail's close calls included soldiers shooting at "our car" and being awakened by a car-bomb exploding at a military outpost next to his hotel: "It blasted my windows out, and big chunks of my ceiling fell down ... while I was in bed, quite the alarm clock," he recalled. Yet he maintains that these events distressed him less than experiencing others' tragedies. "Maybe it would have been different if some of those close calls had been directed at me. But since I knew it was just completely random, and ... I just happened to be nearby it, that was for me a lot less traumatizing than the really tough emotional stories that I got pretty close to" (ibid.).

Witnessing personal anguish was near devastating for both Little and Gold. Little had witnessed a lot of horrific scenes, including "an absolutely ghastly Dante-esque inner circle of hell" in an Iraqi morgue where he and colleague, Marie Colvin, arrived to count people killed by a bomb on an air raid shelter. "Because they had no running water in the morgue and there was nothing to cool it. And these bodies were just piling up, and it was running blood," he said. And at the local hospital, he recalled scores of "horribly mutilated bodies," including "one young woman who had had an awful, catastrophic abdominal wound, and her intestines were spilling out all over the forecourt, a huge, almost like the unfurling of a blanket" (Little 2015).

While distressing, it was damage to the living that was unbearable. "When you see lots of dead people all meshed up there is something unreal about it. It is vile, but they don't seem like real people, as much as living people who have been horribly affected. That's harder to deal with in my view," Little admitted (ibid.).

Wreckage besetting "utterly blameless, decent people who had done nothing wrong" and who were "treated in a most cruel and barbarous way" was emotionally shattering. "They seem less deserving of the cruelty they're suffering when they themselves can manage to be such good people and blameless, [with] acts of kindness in the face of human brutality, who are having the worst time in their lives, and yet still manage to be decent to each other. And I find that very hard [to cope with]," he said (ibid.).

In a 1992 encounter during the Bosnian War, Little vividly remembered an "old couple were living in this bombed-out hotel. It had burned at the start of the war. And they'd found a corner of what had been a function room. The walls were all black with soot, and they were living there as refugees. And there was no glass in the windows, and it was fairly freezing," he recalled. "He talked about the hardships of not being able to get water and being cold at night and getting hungry, not having enough food and the constant threat of the bombs falling all around where he was living and losing his home on the other side of the front-line ... He'd lost everything. And then he said, at the very end, 'The hardest thing though is not being able to communicate with my daughters. They're in Zagreb in Croatia. And I'm sure they don't know whether we're even still alive. And it's horrid. The hardest thing is not having communication with people we love'" (ibid.).

Little planned to travel to Zagreb next, so he offered to deliver a message from the man to his daughters. "He was so excited by this, unbelievably excited ... He wrote, 'Please thank this kind journalist for making this communication. Mummy and I are fine. Please don't worry about us. I know we will soon be drinking coffee together any day.' And I thought, 'no, he doesn't.' He knows he probably won't survive the winter, and it broke my heart. So I remember holding it together to say goodbye to him, but as we were walking down the street, [I was] just falling apart" (ibid.).

In the utter ruin, Little was struck that "the old man was wearing a tie, I remember. He had a tie on. And I mean, why would you in that situation? But you could see he thought, 'no, I'm not going to compromise. I've got to keep up standards.' It was a version of self-dignity" (ibid.).

Shattered lives were more distressing than physical carnage for Gold as well. "It's not [the] gore or something like that [that] hits you hard. It's like, in a refugee camp, and you're talking to a father who's just had to flee his home, [and] he's got two kids, like how to deal with that when he starts breaking down in front of you. That to me is more traumatic than someone getting shot in front of me," he conceded. "Desperate people with no hope and no one to help them is pretty [much] worse ... You see it even in New York. You're seeing, every other day, you're talking to a mother who just lost her son, or a son who just lost his parents, whether it's crime or an accident or a disaster or whatever. A mother losing her son here is the same as a mother losing her son there. Same shit" (Gold 2014).

The losses and tragedies accumulate, overwhelming some journalists to the point of no return. This was the case for PJ09 while covering human trafficking and slavery along the Mexican border. "I would try to be strong, [but] I would go home and just start crying and crying and crying," she recalled. "It [was] just too much. I'm like dying inside. It's just too much" (PJ09 2014).

Her empathic sorrow made it nearly impossible to continue covering the subjects. "I was afraid of being sensitive ... to the stories," she admitted (ibid.).

Delayed Effects

Sometimes trauma is insidious, creeping in and rearing itself long after the incidents. For both Jamail and long-time foreign correspondent Carol Williams, the emotional impact lagged, until after they left the danger zones. "When you are in there, what most people will experience is that [the experience] becomes normalized. And you kind of have to do that to work in there because you have to put on all this emotional armor and just start getting the stories and interviewing people and getting the information you need and just getting the job done," Jamail explained. "This is common with a lot of vets I've spoken with [too] ... You get to where you really can't feel anything anymore but rage or being numb ... Not until I left and came back to the [United] States that I realized, 'oh wow, I'm in a totally different place psychologically than most other folks'" (Jamail 2014).

Williams's emotions welled up upon arriving in Italy to decompress from her assignment in Bosnia. In Sarajevo, she had interviewed a hospitalized young boy who had survived an attack, but was one of many "kids seeing their teachers blown up in front of them [and then] ending up in hospitals with a bunch of fighters talking about how they were going to go and kill the 'Chetniks,'"[1] Williams said. "He was nine years old ... and he was sent to this hospital, and he was in a room with like three or four hardened Muslim fighters who were all wounded ... It was so sad" (Williams 2014; The Scholars' Circle 2012).

While on assignment, Williams felt "okay" and continued reporting as normal and after a month in Bosnia was "so relieved" to leave the war-torn country for Italy. But while "drinking wine and eating my grilled vegetables and waiting for my pasta, I was thinking, 'oh my God, this is such a different life.' And all of a sudden I just erupted into tears, uncontrolled sobbing, just thinking about these poor little kids, who, through no fault of their own, were living this horrible life ... I just kind of lost it" (Williams 2014).

The Effects

Most interviewed foreign correspondents rejected the notion that they suffered serious trauma. Pulitzer Prize-winning journalist Roy Gutman, a veteran of conflict zones, for example, said, "I don't think I've experienced [trauma]. Maybe I have. [But] not in a way that's changed my work capabilities or style or anything else ... I've been in close calls, and I'm usually able to move on ... They do take time to get over sometimes" (Gutman 2014).

ABC News broadcaster Robert Woodruff's was more than a close call. Struck by an improvised explosive device that nearly killed him, Woodruff suffered a brain injury that left him aphasic. But he contends that neither the attack nor his collective war-zone experiences psychologically injured him: "I'm not sure that they really had a major trauma effect on me in all those years" (Woodruff 2014).

PC10 endured several "close calls," including "a barrel bomb that fell like maybe about fifty feet from where we were," and great tragedies—grief, injuries, damaged children. But she, too, downplayed the severity of their effects: "Yeah, yeah, I'm sure if I have some residual PTSD of some sort, I mean ... I don't know if it's PTSD, but there are certain things that trigger memories, especially [in a city] with helicopters always above. That always kind of takes you back because helicopters were what dropped the barrel bombs in Aleppo" (PC10 2014).

Even Szlanko, who endured an abduction in Syria and acknowledged the difficulties and stress of the job, assured me that his experiences were not "leaving me with any disorder ... I don't think it's leaving me with any festering wounds ... I'm not a great believer in this stuff [such as PTSD] to be honest" (Szlanko 2014).

He credits journalists' resilience: "I think a lot of this is down to just how much you can take, stuff like just the extreme violence and how much a person can take. I know a lot of people who are just more solid types who don't kind of talk that much and [are] more patient. And they seem to have stronger nerves, and they're just better at it ... They're just more stable types I suppose. And there are some people who are just not very good at it" (ibid.).

In contrast, Jamail believes that some PTSD is unavoidable for danger zone journalists. "Nobody goes into a war-zone like that and doesn't get PTSD to some degree," he said. "It's a real thing, and it's a thing that most war correspondents are in total denial of because nobody likes to ... It's like, 'Well trauma doesn't really happen to journalists. You have to be a soldier, you know, killing people and that kind of thing for it to happen to [you].' And it's not true" (Jamail 2014).

Two interviewees, including Terry McCarthy, suggested that "a lot of journalists probably don't even realize what they're struggling with ... We've hidden them [emotional issues] a lot ... [and] I think it hasn't really been looked at enough" (The Scholars' Circle 2012).

It may also be that the symptoms are simply too elusive to identify. For example, while Gold acknowledged the stress, but noted, "it's nothing acute, and I can't trace back to particular moments that I have flashes of or visions … [It's] not like the movies. It's not like you have nightmares all the time about your living style and you wake up screaming" (Gold 2014).

Afflictions manifest themselves in "very high divorce rates, on top of alcohol and drug abuse," which is "not very well recognized. Alcohol is always a risk. You have to be aware of that. It's the famous bane of foreign correspondents," explained McCarthy. "This cliché about the hard-drinking war correspondent, a lot of the time I think you can look at the roots of that abuse of alcohol and sometimes drugs from what they've experienced … [It's] self-medicating" (The Scholars' Circle 2012).

Self-medication is one of a few less-than-healthy means of coping, according to interviewees. "If I search my brain, I could find the individual causes of [my] emotions. But I'm conscious of how I've dealt with them, and they're not necessarily healthy ways," admitted Vice News' Editor-in-Chief, Jason Mojica, adding that journalists sometimes "use that lifestyle to justify poor life decisions that are just unhealthy behavior … [and] develop some sort of nihilistic tendencies" (Mojica 2014).

Their own affect and resilience aside, interviewees nearly universally recognized suffering among colleagues. Gutman's colleague in Iraq refused to return to the field after her brush with death. "[She] was close to a checkpoint when a car bomb blew up fairly close by and killed some people. And it could have been her. And she's been traumatized ever since. She's a totally wonderful person with great humor and great skills and so on, but I know we can't send her back to Baghdad. She was supposed to go a few months ago, and she copped out … There was nothing I could do for her, except to say, 'get counseling.' And I think she did, but it didn't work," recalled Gutman. "It happens to journalists just like it happens to soldiers. And it is traumatic stress … especially [after] a close call" (Gutman 2014).

The effects are widespread and affect "a lot of journalists," acknowledged McCarthy. "I have friends who have problems" (The Scholars' Circle 2012). Woodruff agreed, acknowledging "There's tons of traumatic stress disorder, post-traumatic stress that people [journalists] have when they come back. It's a huge part of our world, and that's an absolute reality" (Woodruff 2014).

A New Normal

The work transforms the worker, according to journalists, including Mojica and McCarthy. While McCarthy acknowledges that "The things I've seen over my career make me never want to see another war again," he simultaneously notes the insidious nature of the job. "You don't go into this job to be a war junkie. But the flip side to that is that you become one" (The Scholars' Circle 2012).

That's the "danger," which David Schlesinger of Reuters warns arises when journalists "just want to go all the time and don't rest and don't take care of themselves. I think it is best that you have someone who acknowledges that they're war-weary, who acknowledges that it's been a traumatic experience. That's what you want, someone who's very self-aware, and who'll take care of themselves. What you don't want is someone who just gets so hooked on the adrenaline that they start getting reckless" (Schlesinger 2014).

Addiction aside, working in the field has other effects. It changes one's sense of normality, in addition to attitudes, perspectives, and relationships. "Old ways-of-being just become alien. Ways of relaxing, of enjoying things, and everything seems different because you are different," explained Mojica. "That is how you feel if you spend this much time living in this alternate reality, conflict and crisis" (Mojica 2014).

For example, Mojica still feels "an incredible amount of empathy for the people I'm doing stories about, but ironically that work has made me so much less sympathetic to almost any normal problem that people have. You're coming home and you're like, 'come on, the perspective of it,' which is unfortunate, and it's not fair to people because their problems exist within their life" (ibid.).

The historian and *Al Jazeera* columnist Mark LeVine reported a variation on that theme. "You just become a harder person," he said. "You become less nice of a person. I've been told that by my wife, [that] I'm not as nice as I was 10 or 15 years ago. I don't know if that's true" (The Scholars' Circle 2012).

The inurement, however, serves the craft, according to Mojica. "I've said hundreds of times, I'm cold so that other people can be emotional about these stories. Basically I feel that I'm there to get at those stories, and to push people to tell those stories. You're always dancing on the edge of exploitation: 'I'm here to get you and I'm going to zoom in when you cry,'" he said. "You have to be a bit cold and cynical in order to capture these things or basically be in a place where people are suffering, and I'm going to walk up and I'm going to put this camera really close to you and get a really good shot because that's the thing that will make someone else care. A sense of justification and then a lot of drinking" (Mojica 2014).

For Gold, the work has "definitely affected the way I see things," he said. "I think it makes you a bit more skeptical, more cynical in a lot of ways ... It affects my perception of human nature a lot more ... If you go in there with an idealized view of a situation, you can come out being a little more cynical or skeptical of certain situations as well ... Basically, it makes everything relatively gray. I'd say it's hard to be completely black and white about issues ... You don't put things on a pedestal, or people on a pedestal, or ideas on a pedestal in general" (Gold 2014).

Simultaneously, living in extreme crises reduces interviewed correspondents' own day-to-day anxieties, according to Glazer. "You also sure as hell feel a lot safer here, [un]like everyone who's freaking out about

Ebola or street crime or all these things that people obsess about in America. I feel awfully safe in New York City, always. This looming threat of terrorism that we've been agonizing about since 9/11, I covered that. It was scary, and I lived in New York at the time, and I was there. But I'm not worried about terrorism that way, having lived where you actually have to worry about terrorism. I feel awfully damned safe in my home after being in these places. I feel like my world and our world here is pretty safe and good, and people are good, and that is actually a good by-product of going to these places, to cover bad things" (Glazer 2014).

Mojica agreed. "The experience of these stories from some of the places you wouldn't necessarily take a vacation is what kind of made me less afraid of being a father" because "there are kids in eastern Congo in the jungle, and they're okay, and people grew up there, and they're alive, and they're adults, and … in Afghanistan, where I was like, 'so how hard can this really be?'" (Mojica 2014).

Willingness to engage in everyday distractions can also shift. "Once in a while, I'll talk about stuff like that [sports]" and "regular" subjects, admitted Gold. But he is not "self-righteous" if others want or need them. "That's fine to try and distract yourself" (Gold 2014).

But as normality shifts, other life and career options may fade. "Well you can't really go back," admits Gold. "There's nothing else I could do … because to go back to a nine-to-five job, there's no way in hell I could do it. I wish I could, at times" (ibid.).

Career Trauma

Detentions and proximate attacks "are bad enough," insisted Gutman. But he is more distressed when an important story he found cannot find its way into publication. "What traumatizes me, the one thing that does, is if I've got a really powerful story that I think is really important, and I can't get it into print. I go out of my mind. Because I feel that everything I've done is being held up to question. And I'm not sure how to go on in that circumstance. It's rather hard. And yet you have that too often" (Gutman 2014).

New Zealand freelance journalist, Jon Stephenson recounted the many risks for foreign correspondents, beginning with "the risks on the ground" and of "psychological injury because of the nature of the work and the isolation or the stress or the exposure to deeply traumatizing events." For example, he and his travel mates "got mortared," which he called, "pretty frightening, mainly because it happened so fast. There was so little warning, and the mortar rounds were landing very close," he recalled. "We went up to the frontline … [and] got mortared on the way up. Four vehicles, and we were going round a steep bend, and a mortar round just landed, so we all jumped out of our vehicles, and everyone took cover" (Stephenson 2014).

As a freelance reporter, Stephenson and others in his situation also face "financial stress, and then you work hard to make sure your sources are looked after and protected and that the story's done as well as possible. And you have the risk, I guess, if you want to put it that way, of when it comes out, it won't be given the attention that you think it merits. And that's a risk in itself because you're spending a lot of time on it. And you don't want it to just disappear in tomorrow's fish and chip wrappers" (ibid.).

And still there is another challenge that Stephenson finds most distressing—"the risk that you take by challenging the narrative, the established narrative in your own country. To me that's far and away the most disturbing aspect of my work," he admitted. "Politicians can actively come out to undermine your credibility or destroy your professional reputation because they don't like the story. That's something that is of an altogether different level ... particularly when you've been in a conflict zone, and you come back to a country like New Zealand, which is your home and the place that you want to exhale and feel safe, not just physically but psychologically. I think it's very destabilizing and disconcerting" (ibid.).

The character attacks serve to "intimidate and to shut people down. And it often works. And it often works in the sense that people don't even embark on rocking the boat because they know what may await them because they've seen the lessons, or they've seen the precedents ... the possible fate that awaits them if they rock the boat," argued Stephenson (ibid.).

Dealing with Trauma

"There is no Vets Administration for journalists ... And so you have to look at health programs with individual employers," explained McCarthy (The Scholars' Circle 2012).

Increasingly, media companies recognize the hazards of the job and offer counseling and other programs to their journalists. Interviewees have made use of them. Gold, for example, "started talking to somebody because work paid for it" (Gold 2014).

Gold had noticed long-term effects of field work on correspondents and "didn't want to end up like that," he said. "So I try to process it and see what I can learn, and keep it going because when you keep doing this. You have to" (ibid.).

"Self-care" is part of the hostile environment training programs offered by large media companies. And while "everyone would chuckle at" that component, approximately "85% of everyone agreed that 'this was helpful,'" acknowledged Glazer. But he adds, "It's one of those things that everyone deals with differently. If you lay it out, it can be seen as kind of silly" (Glazer 2014).

Universally, communication was the means by which interviewees dealt with their traumatic experiences, primarily through counseling.

Jamail, for example, found himself "needing to talk with some people about it," he said. "I kind of learned after the fact, after talking to some people that do work with folks, helping them kind of re-assimilate and process things PTSD-related ... And after a little while it worked" (Jamail 2014).

Colleagues have served their needs just as well, according to interviewees. "You try to find other journalists you can talk to about it. It's usually told in the form of anecdotes and war stories, rather than, 'I'm feeling kind of messed up,'" said Glazer. "I felt like I told the story [about the Congo kidnapping] over and over again" (Glazer 2014). Mojica agreed, adding, "They [journalists] are the only ones you can actually have those conversations with, who understand what you're talking about, that you don't have to explain everything" (Mojica 2014).

In contrast, family and friends who can't quite relate may instead react with alarm and worry, which makes matters worse. "You want to talk to somebody about it, but not someone where you're dumping this on them. And they worry, and it reflects back, either then, or [then] you're trying to make them feel better. And then the next time you're trying to do your job, they're affected by that," acknowledged Glazer (2014).

Still, time, place, and audience matter. "I remember at work, a week later [after the abduction], we came in, and we were having a staff meeting, and my boss asked me what happened," recalled Glazer. "He wanted me to tell the story. And that was not helpful to talk to a room full of people about it" (ibid.).

Szlanko processed his abduction ordeal through his work. "When I was kidnapped, that was a big trauma. And how do you deal with trauma? The standard process is to talk about it, just to get it out of your system. And I did that. What I did was I sat down, and I wrote down the whole thing for myself. In minute detail. Down to the smallest emotion. I wrote down everything, everything that I remembered. Everything. Absolutely everything. There was not one thing that I didn't write down that I remembered. And that for me was helpful. And until I did that, I was sleeping pretty badly. I had difficulty sleeping for the first few days, and I had bad dreams. But once I'd done that, it was fine. And I never thought about it again. This is what psychologists will do as well if you get into one of these PTSD programs. The main thing is to talk about it. My understanding is that the most supportive process for dealing with trauma is talk about it. Just to get it out of your system" (Szlanko 2014).

Writing heals through expurgation, according to Szlanko. "In my experience, journalists deal with these things fairly well, and I think the reason for that is that they're filters. Stuff comes in and then goes out the other end," he said. "They write it out of themselves and that helps digest it. You can go and see these things, destroyed houses and dead people and things like that, and then you write. I always find it helpful. If you're going to ask me point blank, 'do you have nightmares?' No, I don't, because all that stuff goes out at the other end. And I think that process of digesting it and pushing it out is extremely helpful in that regard ... I think there's a lot you can do yourself. Sort of talk about it and write about it" (ibid.).

Leaving danger zones for more peaceful ground is the other well-practiced strategy, according to interviewees, giving foreign correspondents a "chance to decompress," said Schlesinger (2014).

While Gutman served as *McClatchy News'* Foreign Editor in Baghdad, foreign correspondents worked for five to six weeks before taking a three-week break for decompression. "It sounds good on paper, but it turns out it wasn't long enough because you need extra rest to get over what you've been seeing and doing and hearing," particularly after a harrowing experience, when he insisted reporters "have time off immediately" (Gutman 2014).

After a series of danger zone assignments, McCarthy took a long-term assignment in Tokyo, which he described as "very peaceful ... I did three years in Japan, three and a half years in Japan, and that weaned me off a lot of the trauma from South East Asia" (McCarthy 2014).

Other antidotes include seeing friends, playing sports and getting service animals, according to interviewees. "Getting a dog just kind of opens your heart back up, and that's why you see these stories about vets working with dogs ... especially the guys with really severe PTSD," said Jamail. "Long after I left Iraq in '06 and '07 and [I was] still doing stories from back in the States, and I'd come across a real tough piece of information, or learned that another one of my Iraqi friends got killed or something like that, [I would] go lay down on the bed ... and the dog would just come up and know you're in distress and would just come and hang out with you ... Over time with that kind of thing happening consistently, it just kind of opens you back up. For me anyway that's how it really helped" (Jamail 2014).

Despite challenges, exposure to the others' pain reminds journalists of their own privileges. "I feel privileged because I have the opportunity to go find my stories, document my stories, my videos and have the opportunity to come back to my family in a safe place," said Claudia Nunez to the Los Angeles Press Club. "A lot of my colleagues in Mexico, they don't have this privilege. It is a horrible situation" (The Scholars' Circle 2012).

Local danger zone journalists who seek refuge in safer countries still face hurdles with their traumas. "My [Mexican] colleagues are here [in the USA] as undocumented people. [They] suffer with stress, depression, a lot of mental issues, and they don't have the right to go and look for assistance. Others are in detention center, federal detention center. Let me tell you, a federal detention center is just hell. You basically are victimized," explained Nunez. "You stay there for months without contact with family, so after all that, you suffer. You go in this detention center and wait for six, seven, eight months by yourself in a jail. Why? Because you looked for a better life. You looked for refuge. This option is not available for Mexican journalists" (ibid.).

Interviewees are aware of the harrowing conditions for local danger zone journalists. "[It's] much, much greater than for any foreign journalist," said Schlesinger (2014). The story of local danger zone journalists follows in Chapter 5, "Living in a Danger Zone."

Note

1 Chetniks were extreme nationalist Serbs.

References

Glazer, Andrew. 2014. Personal Interview. In Person. Brooklyn, NY. October 31.
Gold, Danny. 2014. Personal Interview. In Person. Brooklyn, NY. October 31.
Gutman, Roy. 2014. Personal Interview. Via Skype. Auckland to Istanbul. December 6.
Jamail, Dahr. 2014. Personal Interview. Via Telephone. November 10.
Little, Allan. 2015. Personal Interview. Via Telephone. Auckland to London. January 27.
McCarthy, Terry. 2014. Personal Interview. In Person. Los Angeles. July 7.
Mojica, Jason. 2014. Personal Interview. In Person. Brooklyn, NY. October 31.
PC10. 2014. Personal Interview. In Person. Site withheld. November 11.
PJ09. 2014. Personal Interview. In Person. Site withheld. November 10.
Schlesinger, David. 2014. Personal Interview. Via Skype. Los Angeles to Hong Kong. November 27.
The Scholars' Circle. 2012. "Reporting from the Danger Zone." Panel Discussion. First broadcast September 30.
Stephenson, Jon. 2014. Personal Interview. In Person. Auckland, NZ. December 12.
Szlanko, Balint. 2013. "My Harrowing Kidnapping Ordeal in Syria." *The Daily Beast*. January 29. http://www.thedailybeast.com/articles/2013/01/29/my-harrowing-kidnapping-ordeal-in-syria.html. Accessed March 26, 2016.
Szlanko, Balint. 2014. Personal Interview. Via Skype. November 12.
Williams, Carol. 2014. Personal Interview. In Person. Los Angeles. June 26.
Woodruff, Bob. 2014. Personal Interview. Via Telephone. Los Angeles to New York. November 13.

4 Staying Alive

It makes it really difficult to do your job when all sides regard you as fair game, and at best, you're in the way, and you're taking pictures of them doing things they shouldn't be doing.

Carol Williams, *Los Angeles Times*

The job—covering war, corruption, organized crime or authoritarian governments—is naturally dangerous, as power rarely enjoys scrutiny. Historically, in the risk-versus-benefit analysis, decisions tended toward taking risks to tell important stories. During the 1990s, for example, Michael Parks, then deputy foreign editor at the *Los Angeles Times*, supported correspondents' desires over cautious objections from the foreign editor. "We were working on a series at the [*Los Angeles*] *Times* … on Mujahedin who had fought the Soviets in Afghanistan, and then had scattered back to the various countries they had come from," he recalled. "And I agreed with the correspondent, John-Thor Dahlburg, that he could go into Afghanistan to meet, essentially, with the Taliban. He walked in and walked out, and we didn't have a lot of communication with him when he was there" (Parks 2014).

Parks also approved Dahlburg's coverage in Algeria, "a very dangerous place, both for Westerners and for journalists. He was both. We talked about how he was going to get in, what he was going to do, whether it was worth it. And we decided it was, and he went in. We were in touch through that daily, and he told me what he was doing, and we got him out. He flew in, legally, with his American passport" (ibid.).

Even in the 1990s, decades before the rise of journalist abductions and gruesome murders, risks were high enough for Parks to prepare his correspondents for the worst case scenarios, asking them questions such as, "'Have you got your shots? Where's your will? Does anybody know where it is?' I remember telling Mark Fineman, who was going off to Baghdad, I said, 'Okay, so where's the will?' He told me. And I said … 'One last thing, Michelle (his wife) knows you're doing this, right?' 'Yeah, yeah.' I said, 'Does your mother know? Your mother gets the *L.A. Times*, and she's going to see that her Jewish boy is in Baghdad in the center of a war. You better call your mother, Mark'" (ibid.).

Journalists often operated with a non-combatant status, in which they could safely navigate conflict zones. During the civil wars in El Salvador, for example, Terry McCarthy recalls driving "from San Salvador, the capital of El Salvador, which was in the control of the government. [You'd] drive into the highlands and meet the guerillas and talk to them, and you'd drive back and talk to the government again, and that wasn't sanctionable. The government didn't go after journalists who tried to do that. Since 9/11 that non-combatant status for journalists has pretty much evaporated" (McCarthy 2014).

Before the twenty-first century's turmoil, the Yugoslav Wars grew unexpectedly perilous, catching even senior journalists by surprise when combatants turned their guns onto them. "We presumed that we were perceived as neutral observers of the conflict and not aligned with any particular party," remembered Carol Williams. "Those things can change so quickly. One incident of somebody saying, 'Well, the other side came in and started shooting up your village because they saw the journalists were there.' Then suddenly we become the beacons for difficulties and problems. And there's resentment, and they start targeting us" (The Scholars' Circle 2012).

The wars of the former Yugoslavia took some two dozen journalists' lives and wounded 33 (Helsinki Watch 1992), a startling number at the time. "The paper had not covered anything quite like this, and they just didn't know," said Roy Gutman. "Most news organizations hadn't done something where … there was no protective power. There was really no one you could go to who was going to shelter you. So you didn't really know what the risks were … Every time you left the hotel in Sarajevo, you could be fired on … It happened in many places … [But] assuming nothing happens, you just move on, you say, 'Okay, that was that for the day'" (Gutman 2014).

Today, even compared to the "open season" on journalists in the former Yugoslavia, the threats are staggering. "In the Yugoslav war, where I spent nearly four years, you could go over to the Serb side almost all the time, even when NATO was threatening to bomb, and you could get around. You would be restricted and humiliated, intimidated and so on, but you could go there without being worried that you'd end up with your throat cut. You can't do that now [in today's war-zones]," explained Veteran BBC correspondent Allan Little (Little 2015).

Today's threats have changed the equation for even the most seasoned journalists. Little elaborated, "The main danger [then] was being caught in crossfire, being in the wrong place at the wrong time. And enough of my friends were killed for that to be no small thing at the time. But it was nothing compared, well it wasn't nothing, but it was of a smaller magnitude than the risks that are being run now and the obstacles that puts in our way" (ibid.).

ABC News broadcaster Robert (Bob) Woodruff agreed and reflected upon the changes. "In the old days, if you put your TV or journalism tape on your vehicle, people wouldn't attack you because you're telling them you're a journalist," he said. "If the so-called enemies wanted to make their point, they want to tell it to you as a journalist, so you could tell their story as well. You were their way to send out a message. [But now] I think the message that they want to send is that every single one of us is vulnerable, and they could kill us at any time. And I think that is what the insurgents have now done ... Now they love it when you're a journalist. You've seen that, especially ISIS, so I think they have a different tactic" (Woodruff 2014).

Before the rise of powerful insurgencies who were hostile to journalists and determined to use them for their own purposes, Afghanistan and Iraq seemed "still safe" for journalists, said Woodruff. "After the bombing ended in Afghanistan itself, and the US forces ultimately moved in, at that time, the Taliban started to hide or disappear. They were not really a major force in most of the places where we were, so we were able to wander around somewhat in this first year or so. In Iraq, it was really the same" (ibid.). But today, journalists are a "big get" for insurgents, particularly if the journalist is "someone from the US, or any of the NATO countries," he said (ibid.).

Veteran reporter Carol Williams elaborated: "[We are] not only not perceived as independent and neutral. We're prizes. If the insurgents can grab you and make an example of you, that's a feather in their cap" (The Scholars' Circle 2012).

Mounting dangers and rampant lawlessness have prevented journalists from reporting in many regions of Afghanistan and Iraq. "The only territory in Afghanistan that was accessible was the territory that's controlled securely by Western-backed governments. So you could fly to Herat from Kabul. [But] you can't drive there. It's a bit like parts of the United States after the Civil War," explained Little (2015).

Syria is another out-of-range country for most correspondents. "Almost no one is going over the border into Aleppo," said Woodruff. "Not many people want to go down there either, because you can't figure out how to defend yourself. I'm not sure being extremely experienced to go amongst an ISIS area is going to decrease the ... risk of you being there. I think it's kind of a roll of the dice in some of those places now" (Woodruff 2014).

Media companies, such as Reuters and the BBC, have withdrawn from covering these hotspots, particularly ISIS-controlled regions of Syria, and are declining coverage more frequently. "You can just see what's happening with ISIS for example, where journalists are—it's horrific. [Journalists are] not seen as someone who can chronicle the story. They're seen as someone who can be used as a pawn in the story. I think that clearly as an editor you have to say, 'no, I'm not going to have my people put in a situation where they could be taken prisoner or hostage,'" said David Schlesinger, former Editor-in-Chief of Reuters news agency (Schlesinger 2014).

While media organizations, such as the BBC, maintained journalists nearby, in Lebanon and Turkey, they refused to allow them to cross into more dangerous regions. "They're not pulling people out because there's nobody there in the first place. It's a question about how far to push people in," said Little (2015).

With today's new perils, Parks acknowledged that he would also reject requests by journalists planning to enter Syria, which two years ago, he approved. "It wasn't as bad as it is now ... I would have said 'no' if it were now." And while journalists bemoan the lack of access, most agree with Parks's assessment—"No story is worth anybody's life, certainly not mine" (Parks 2014).

While interviewed correspondents lament restrictions, they also reject unnecessary risk-taking and criticize journalists who needlessly expose themselves to danger. For example, "You have the case of this crazy guy, this American writer, who had spent time in Yemen," recalled Gutman. "He was in Antakya, looking for a way into Syria and met up with some people he knew were Islamists. And he said [that] he wanted to write their story. And he went in there totally unprepared. And he was arrested immediately. He escaped because he was held by Nusra, and Nusra decided to let him go about six months ago. And he wrote a story ... But this guy is out of his mind. He's loopy because he was taking chances so far beyond what anybody would do with a head on their shoulders" (Gutman 2014).

In addition to their own well-being, concerns about the safety of their sources prevent entry, according to historian and *Al Jazeera* columnist Mark LeVine. "If you go as the Westerner into Iraq or going into Pakistan, you want to help uncover the reality and share it with the world, but of course you're putting a lot of people's lives in danger that are working with you. And I've been dying to get back to Iraq for years, but all of my friends there say, 'Please don't come. It's too dangerous for you to come back.' And I sympathize because I remember how bad it was being there ... But of course, what does that do to the story if you can't get back?" (The Scholars' Circle 2012).

Hidden Dangers

Hardly anyone in the profession realized just how bad it really was, and so they continued as normal. "No one was talking about [the extent of the kidnappings and killings]," acknowledged Jason Mojica, Vice News Editor-in-Chief. "If you were operating within certain circles, people knew that was happening. But half of the journalists didn't know that was happening," partially due to "a media blackout around the kidnapping[s]", leaving unsuspecting journalists to "keep walking into a meat grinder basically ... People [didn't] know there was a problem, and then it becomes a plague of kidnapping[s]" (Mojica 2014).

As word spread about the spate of abductions, journalists still mis-understood the perpetrators' identities and their locations. Hungarian freelance journalist Balint Szlanko, for example, proceeded as normal until he was seized. "This was in January 2013. This is before the big wave of kidnappings started, which really started in the Spring of last year [2014]. There had been kidnappings before, and James Foley had gone missing a few months before that. Another American journalist, Austin Tyse, had gone missing half a year before," he said, but at the time, "the working hypothesis that we had was that these people had been taken by the [Bashar al Assad] regime, which we now know is not true. They were taken by somebody else. But at the time there was no really visible threat from the rebels. Our assumptions were that the rebels were okay. There are some groups that you had to be careful with, and you best stay clear of some groups, and we knew it was chaotic. And we knew there was warlordism, and there were dangerous people around. But we didn't really assume that [they were behind the abductions]" (Szlanko 2014).

As the extent of the dangers grew apparent, the decisions became clearer: Stay out of territory controlled by extremist groups such as the Islamic State or the Taliban. After three journalists on their way to Kabul were pulled from their vehicles and shot dead, reportedly by the Taliban, "that had the sort of effect that a lot of people, who had been going in, would have pulled out, so it was like a giant vacuum cleaner sort of suc-tioned all the Western journalists out of that area for a while," said New Zealand freelance journalist Jon Stephenson who was in Pakistan at the time (Stephenson 2014).

After a Vice News journalist was nabbed by a rebel group al Nusra, the group with which he had planned to embed, the company scrapped its planned production there. "David Enders … was going to embed with al Nusra Front before they had declared their allegiance to Al Qaeda. He had gone and set it up with the big boss, and while coming back, he got grabbed," recalled Mojica. "This is 2012, [he was] kidnapped with the guy he was working with, thrown in trunk and [he] desperately tried to convince them, 'no, I was just meeting with your boss.' And after about seven hours, he finally managed to convince them, 'no really, I was. Here are all the names, all the commanders.' It was the lower ranking guys [who abducted him]. So we decided that it wasn't the safest things for us to do" (Mojica 2014).

Szlanko—well-versed in the Middle East—steered clear of ISIS-controlled regions because, he said, "If you're facing an organization like ISIS who is hunting journalists, there's really very little you can do frankly, which is why a lot of people don't go to Syria anymore. I don't. I've been to Syria three times since, but I went to very different areas, very different local dynamics. I haven't been anywhere near ISIS-controlled areas since, and again, at the time, ISIS wasn't around. There was no ISIS to the best of our knowledge. I had heard the name ISIS much later for the first time. If

I'd known there was an organization in town hunting for foreign journalists, I wouldn't have gone anywhere near Aleppo" (Szlanko 2014).

Gutman also "stopped going" into ISIS-held territories "because they had publicly warned that they were going to kidnap journalists and detain journalists, and it was well known. Other people who went in afterwards, I don't understand why they would've, why they would've ignored the warnings" (Gutman 2014).

In lieu of investigating the most hostile forces, such as ISIS, interviewed journalists settled on other important stories that required less risk. Admittedly, however, "there's always the risk of being shot at and winding up in a fire fight, or being bombed by the regime. But if you're with people who realize you want to tell their story, and certainly the rebel forces, the moderate rebel forces, do, you can do a lot of things with reasonable safety," explained Gutman (ibid.).

For example, Gutman focused on the plight of internally displaced people at the Syrian border "who were living in tents or even under the stars [in] huge numbers, who nobody was really paying attention to, and I just thought I could try to put them in the spotlight, and I did two, I thought, very strong stories," he said (ibid.).

The trip was nonetheless cut short for safety concerns. "It was only a one-day trip. And we were going to go in a second day from another border crossing, but we decided it was too unsafe. And the people who were escorting us could not give us an assurance," said Gutman (ibid.).

Vice News' Danny Gold remained in Kurdish-held regions of Iraq and Syria "because I knew it was relatively safe" and "because I knew I could trust them, and I could be protected," he said, adding that he would readily return upon assignment (Gold 2014).

Should I Stay or Should I Go?

It's always a "calculation and a tradeoff" on everything, considering the necessity of the risks of the story against its "potential benefits" said interviewees (Gold 2014; Schlesinger 2014; Williams 2014). "If you're going to drive through a hundred miles of hellaciously dangerous territory to go interview a poet about how culture has changed in the midst of war, then it doesn't make any sense," explained Williams (The Scholars' Circle 2012).

Williams avoided high-risk but low-reward regions, such as the "road-blocks on all the country roads where all you see are a handful of very skittish, drunk, nationalists who've come in from Russia." She also thought "outside the box" when moving "from point A to point B, and in the middle it's very dangerous ... you take three times as long to drive around and go through areas where there's less risk" (Williams 2014).

Still, she pursued interviews at the newly created "regional government headquarters" in Donetsk, which had been erected behind "fortresses that the rebels have created." That was hard enough: "When you do manage to talk yourself into the arms of the rebels, you're in their territory, and you're thinking, 'Is this the time when the Ukrainian government is going to airstrike this building?'" she explained (ibid.)

Nearly every interviewed journalist repeated a version of this equation when choosing their stories. Schlesinger, for example, said, "You're always weighing up the news value of a story against the danger of doing that story, the physical danger to the journalist or the danger to your sources. You always have to weigh that up" (Schlesinger 2014).

While Parks was editor at the *Los Angeles Times*, he "sent them in when they were willing to do things that I thought were worth it," adding that, "As you get more experienced, you know what's worth it" (Parks 2014).

Editors and reporters often disagree on the decision, a process described by Little as a "continual push me-pull you relationship between the teams in the field and the desk back at home, making judgments" (Little 2015).

Still, Little argued that decisions, particularly from the safety of the home office, are colored by unknowns. "Quite often you don't know what you're going to get until you do it." As an example, he described, "There's one team that has been going into Syria from the beginning, and they were quite frustrated because they believed they had a chance to get into a hot part of Syria, and the desk would say, 'No, it's too risky, you can't go.' Or, 'You can't go yet'" (Little 2015).

The calculation differs for print journalists and for photographers or videographers. Print journalists "don't have to have bullets whizzing over our heads to be able to tell our story. In fact, that becomes a cliché that readers don't really want to know about that much," argued Gutman. "Obviously for a photographer, you have no choice but to try to get as close to the action as possible because the drama of the photos makes, often it sells the stories that we write. But it was not a hard decision in a way to try to, on the whole, measure and minute my exposure to sniping and to barrages simply because it didn't really add to my story to operate on that basis" (Gutman 2014).

For this reason Dahr Jamail tucked his camera away, turning to the less conspicuous pen and paper. "It became increasingly difficult to use any kind of a camera because people just didn't want their pictures taken, and it got really, really dangerous ... I even used my little pocket video camera less and less because it became so dangerous, and so I just had a pen and a pad, which are two things very easy to hide and so that's how I went about that ... I really applaud those people that toted the cameras around and the video cameras and such and did that work because it's really, really challenging, and I think in a lot of ways even more dangerous" (Jamail 2014).

Even videographers avoid the most dangerous regions, "where the heaviest fighting is happening," according to Szlanko. In the conflict along the border of Turkey and Syria, correspondents were "watching the war from the other side, from Turkey, and there weren't real dangers. Ukraine was dangerous because it's a conventional mechanized war, and there was a lot of shelling and what not. But we all do the same thing" (Szlanko 2014).

During the war in Afghanistan, however, Stephenson did go to the frontlines. "I was with an American woman journalist, and we went up to the frontline together one day with a commando," he recalled. "We got mortared on the way up. Four vehicles, and we were going round a steep bend, and a mortar round just landed, so we all jumped out of our vehicles, and everyone took cover. We were in ditches ... but then everybody decided to [go back], and I decided to keep going on foot. She looked at me and said, 'Do you think it's safe?' And I said, 'We are in a war-zone. Nothing is safe. If you want safety, go down the mountain.' And she did, much to her credit. And I went running up the mountain on my own ... thinking, 'Why am I doing this?'" (Stephenson 2014).

After the American journalist left, the extent of the risks set in: "Holy crap, what am I doing?" he asked himself. "I could be running across a minefield," or "there could be a sniper here ... Americans could bomb this by mistake ... I could get a leg blown off, and I would be looking back thinking, 'What the hell did I do?' This could be really dumb ... I still remember my heart was pounding, really pounding, and we got to a place where it was very close to the frontline" (ibid.).

In retrospect, Stephenson realized, "It took a lot of courage, actually, for that woman ... That was really mature; she went back down." But at the time, his desire to know more pushed him forward. "I didn't keep running because I wanted to be courageous. I was really curious. I wanted to know, and I wanted to get closer to it ... I just kept going" (ibid.).

A Turning Point

In 2003, Woodruff and his crew felt "safe enough" to report unembedded from Iraq, using local staff and a private security firm. But in 2004, unpredictable violence and chaos engulfed the country. "There looked like there was a new strategy, and new tactics were being adopted by those within Iraq itself," he recalled. "They were starting to blast and blow IEDs and bombing mosques, and we saw the development of the Shiite-Sunni battle ... So after that, people felt largely safe mostly when they embedded with US military units" (Woodruff 2014).

The same chaos forced Jamail to shift strategies. "It wasn't so bad my first trip ... Literally, we would just go out drive around all day and walk around and talk English in public. [Then] you know, it just wasn't a problem, but that changed quickly." By Spring of 2004 conditions had "spun out of control ... Kidnappings started to become widespread, and beheadings and all that. And that's when obviously, I got even more concerned and started becoming a whole lot more careful and a lot more strategic about how we went about doing things ... My interpreter would come pick me up at my hotel, and we'd drive around the block a couple of times to make sure we weren't being followed and then started zipping out, doing a couple of interviews that we'd had set up and then zipping me back in" (Jamail 2014).

Post-2003 Middle East reporting meant that "you can only really afford to dash in and dash out again; you can't hang around in one place for very long because word gets around, and then you're a target," explained Little. "One of the reasons my colleague Frank Darber got shot in Saudi Arabia, I think, was that he and his camera man were noticed. They were in Riyadh of all places, and he and his cameraman were noticed by somebody who was sympathetic to the jihadis in that complex and they phoned and said, 'Listen there's a British TV crew standing on the corner of such and such a street', and five men turned up in a car and shot them. And the cameraman was killed and Frank was paralyzed for life, left for dead in the sand. So the truth is, you've got to get in and get out. You can't go to somebody's house now and sit for three and a half hours and really get their story. You can't hang around a café for three hours listening to people anymore. You've got to get in, get something, and get out again, get away to safety, get back to your guarded compound, whereas in 2003, we could get in our cars and go pretty much anywhere we liked. Even then" (Little 2015).

The Middle East was not the only region that rapidly turned for the worst. PJ09 had been covering the border region between Mexico and the USA for more than a decade. For most of that time, she "could go to Tijuana and cover an education issue or immigration," she said. But things changed drastically when cartels took control of the region and warned her away from territory she had historically covered. "[I received] an order that I can[not] cross ... [that] I cannot go that particular way after like five o'clock" (PJ09 2014). When she asked for a reason, the response came back, "Now, another business [is] in charge [here]," she recalled (ibid.). The border had changed, and had restricted PJ09's access, she acknowledged (ibid.).

The cartels and their violence simultaneously silenced her sources. "People are afraid to talk. You can't go to the mothers, the fathers ... You can't interview families because they are afraid." And sometimes, "their kids are the ones who are the killers. You have 13-year-old(s), 12-year-old(s) who are the killers" (ibid.).

Institutional trust was shattered, damaging journalists' ability to safely deliver information. "You can't go to the police department. They don't provide any protection because they work for the cartels ... You can't trust anyone when you cover this [area]" (ibid.).

The "anyone" applies to friends and colleagues, she added. As Mexico spiraled into worse lawlessness, PJ09 found that journalists and friends had become informants and recruiters for the cartels, ostensibly out of necessity. "I have friends who actually, they had to, they had to do it. It's not an option. Or you're dead … If the guy from the cartel wants to meet with a journalist, the journalists who work with them have to send an invitation … But it's not an invitation … It's a summons" (PJ09 2014).

In a few cases, she believes that journalists "who cover the beat, violence of the police" were seduced by financial rewards. "They all get together, and they all receive money … And if you publish something that [they] don't like, they … hit you, in the back," explained PJ09. "I have friends actually, women friends who had to escape from a window, from a window in the kitchen and [who ran] with her kids because they want[ed] to kill her. I have [another] friend … who had to be there and see what's happening to the other one [as a warning that] … if you don't follow the instructions, then you're going to be the next one" (ibid.).

Rapid Change

Danger zones change rapidly. "It's such a work in progress, how you operate in areas of chaos," according to Williams. "You really have to be on your toes and make a daily, hourly reassessment of what's the best way to proceed and not put yourself in danger, because most of us are not inclined to go and get in between two hails of bullets. It's also not the best way to cover the story" (The Scholars' Circle 2012).

"You're constantly thinking, 'am I going to get kidnapped here?' And you've got to. You've got to be constantly thinking that," added Little (2015). Even with the protection of an armed group, split-second, reflexive decisions can mean life or death. "Friends of mine who were in northern Iraq, going out with the Peshmerga to the frontline, seeing how close they could get to the ISIS frontline. And the risk that they were running was the unpredictability of the northern Iraq Peshmerga. One of them said to me, 'You never know when the Peshmerga are going to turn on their heels and run.' And if they do that, you've got to make sure you're with them. Because if you're not, you get left behind" (ibid.).

Details that may normally be ignored in the past serve as signs about what lies ahead. "You learned how to read a road: Are there kids out playing? That's usually the first sign that something really bad is going on, if the kids are not there. What are the animals doing, particularly the dogs? Is nobody on the road? What is on the side of the road? Are there rocks? In South Africa you look for rocks on the side of the road because they may be thrown," explained Parks (2014).

The Company You Keep

The company journalists keep—colleagues, guides, or host groups—can protect or imperil, according to interviewees. Parks suggested that journalists "learn to travel with somebody, preferably one person with whom you get along [and] who's not got a death wish" (Parks 2014).

Parks avoided traveling with risk-inclined colleagues, including one from Reuters whom he considered "dangerous ... a crazy German. He just took [unnecessary] chances." He avoided another who was "just doing stupid things ... In Vietnam [he] climbed up on the top of, I think it was an [armored] personnel carrier, a vehicle, to get a better view of a battle ... a guy in a white shirt on top of an [armored] personnel carrier" (ibid.).

Woodruff concurred, reiterating the need to seek "people that have experience in those particular areas and those that have had experience in violent spots in the world," and who avoid doing "things that are stupid" (Woodruff 2014).

A traveling companion and the two-car rule was Gutman's formula. The companion in the second car served as backup, particularly in Iraq. "You never go out in one car ... You need a second car in case you have a breakdown because who knows who's going to come along and offer you a lift. And what do you do if you're at risk? And that's a practice that occurred" (Gutman 2014).

One interviewee intentionally avoids colleagues as a means of remaining inconspicuous to hostile authorities. PC10 slips surreptitiously in and out of danger zones, mostly on her own and instead develops a rapport with the local people, who act as her sources, her hosts and guides. "I've been into Syria during the war, I think, nine times. Sometimes it was [with] activists; sometimes with different groups; sometimes with a civilian guide. Each trip is different," she said. "In Syria I have direct contact with the rebels and the activists" who "help me do my job ... the people who [I] met like two years ago I'm still in touch with, and they are now with these rebel groups. I'll go to them because I have an established relationship with them" (PC10 2014).

Through the trust built in those relationships, PC10 develops new sources and hosts. "It was the same way in Libya where it was, you find someone that you trust, and then you sort of transfer that trust," she said, admitting that "it still could have ended very badly, but you sort of know you are making a leap either way. And then, once you establish trust with somebody, they can link you up with somebody else, and then that just sort of grows" (ibid.).

Among the most important company that foreign correspondents keep are their paid local guides, also called "fixers." They provide transportation, insight, translation, and the logistics that ensure safety. But they have also led journalists into adversities.

Local Guides

Horab, the Vice News team's local guide, may have saved their lives in Congo. They had hired local "motorcycle guys" to transport them through the Congolese jungles to meet with Mai-Mai rebels, "one of the main militia groups operating within eastern Congo. And we had gone to basically some sort of UN checkpoint, and that was literally where the road ended. There were UN earthmovers. And the road stopped, and the UN troops wouldn't go any further than that," recalled Mojica (2014).

To reach the Mai-Mai rebels, the production team had to travel another six miles, according to Mojica. "We had to go past the UN jurisdiction into the end of the Congolese military jurisdiction and then to find these rebels in the bush who were known for believing [that] you can have superpowers and can make themselves invisible ... So we hired these motorcycle guys, [and] we were each on the back of a motorcycle making this journey through almost impassable terrain" (ibid.).

That's where they encountered a surprise. "We stumbled upon a group that we thought were the Congolese military, but ended up being the FDLR [Forces Démocratiques de Liberation du Rwanda/Democratic Forces for the Liberation of Rwanda], the Rwandan associated, like Hutu Power rebels. No one was aware that they were there in that area. We weren't expecting to run into them. And they were not happy to see us" (ibid.).

The broadcast crew watched anxiously while Horab negotiated with the rebels to spare them. "We have a little bit of this recording where Horab is basically saying to them that they shouldn't kill us. We're just standing there, nervously, basically knowing that something bad is happening. And Horab, our super-fixer managed to convince them to not kill us," recalled Mojica (ibid.)

At the end of negotiations, the rebels reversed course and instead offered to help. "They ended up providing us with an escort to find the Mai-Mai, which was also terrifying, because it was a journey that was supposed to take an hour and a half. Then after 14 hours, through the dead of night, we finally arrived. We were being led by the Hutu rebels through the dark, and the only reason that we didn't think they were going to kill us was because the walk was so long. And we thought, if they were going to kill us, they would've killed us already. Why would they go through all this trouble? Anyway, it all turned out okay" (ibid.).

In the Northern al Hasakah region of Syria, Gutman's local guide came to the rescue, after a rebel group arrested the journalist and his photographer. "I had a brilliant 'fixer'" who talked the group into releasing the two and their equipment. "There's nothing more valuable than a good fixer in [that] situation ... This guy, he's from one of the tribes there. So all the tribes know all the other tribes ... He had the knowledge of just how to cool them down. The guy's a genius. So he knew what to do ... You try to go with really good people. And you warn them about what is going to go on, and what the risks are, and you try to keep your cool. And you let them play their role as best they can. And you pray that somebody gets it right. So we got out of there that day, which was quite a miracle" (Gutman 2014).

The same guide had also secured the official visas from each region's controlling group, including rebels, which were instrumental in securing their release. "He went to ISIS ... and he asked them, 'Is it permitted for us to travel this route? Because we go through your checkpoints, and we want to get past them, and we want to see what's going on in the east.' And he found somebody. They took our names, they put them on the pass, and so on. And so we had a pass," recalled Gutman (ibid.).

When Gutman wanted to interview displaced Syrians along the border of Turkey, his guide worked for months to protect him from being sold to extremists. "He wanted to be sure that we went in with people who really would risk their lives to protect us, and who would not sell us to the Islamic State, or to anybody else" (ibid.).

In Iraq, Jamail used a different local guide for each region to ensure safety, "especially as the occupation grew on and the sectarianism really was amplified," he said. "In a Sunni area unless you have a Sunni guy with you from that area that has contacts there or a Shia [in a Shia region], or whatever. So if you wanted to go to a certain town, you damn well better have someone from that town" (Jamail 2014).

The local guides' knowledge of the regional dynamics and terrain unequivocally prevent journalists from becoming casualties, according to McCarthy. "We cannot function without them ... Many times they are the people who save your lives. And I've gone through situations where without a local fixer, something very, very bad could have happened. They understand the local situation, and they'll tell you 'Terry get out now', and if you don't listen to them you're very foolish. So all I can do is take off my hat to all those many thousands of unnamed men and women who have helped us get stories out from some very, very dangerous parts of the world" (The Scholars' Circle 2012).

As circumstances have grown too dangerous for foreign correspondents, local guides sometimes perform the actual reporting duties. "There were many times in Iraq when we just couldn't go to places where something had happened, and our local staff would go. I was at ABC at the time, and we lost a cameraman and a sound man precisely for that reason. That they had gone out and got caught in something and were killed," explained McCarthy. "So it behooves us all to remember [when] you see the Western bylines in your newspapers or on your TV screens, behind journalists' bylines are many locals who can be incredibly brave and who are motivated sometimes by money, but also a lot of these people, they really want to get that story out because their country is going through tremendously tough times. And they know that their own government is not going to do it—be it Bashar al Assad or Al Qaeda or whoever it might be. And so they come to Western news organizations very bravely to help us out ... You're seeing the same thing happening in Syria now where Syrians are passing information out because they want somebody to help them fix it. I have huge respect for all these local fixers whose names are never known" (ibid.).

In contrast, "fixers" can also cause trouble, which happened to Andrew Glazer. "I actually had a fixer betray me once in Congo. I wound up getting arrested and then kidnapped the next day ... It was actually the driver, who a fixer that was sort of a last minute add-on, had introduced me to" (Glazer 2014).

Glazer and his team had been investigating a mining site in Congo. Unbeknownst to the correspondents, "the driver had family and friends who worked at the mine ... He tipped them off, so yes, you have to be very careful, and sometimes you get used to trusting people. That's the only time that's happened, and I don't know what I would've done differently to be honest. We were in a place where there was no one to really help us out, and we took who we could get, and obviously, we picked a bad one" (ibid.).

Both the driver and local guide were referrals of another local guide, "a fantastic fixer" in an earlier production. The earlier guide was "arrested with us, and he felt equally betrayed," recalled Glazer. "It's a thing if you're going to a big city or a place where there [is] some sort of infrastructure. There's other places where you're just in the middle of the bush in Congo, and it's hard to check someone's background or vet them" (ibid.).

In the worst cases, "fixers are the new jailers. You know the story of Anthony Loyd, the British reporter, in Syria, where his fixer was basically preparing to sell him to ISIS. And he escaped with his life. It was really not a happy thing. He had people he knew and trusted inside of Syria," said Gutman. "And there's warnings out now about the way, both in Kobane and in Gaziantep, and maybe even in Antakya, I've heard for all those places, that there are fixers who are out to capture Western journalists and sell them to ISIS" (Gutman 2014).

Hiring local guides on a full-time basis onto the news organizations' staff is the safest bet, according to Gutman. "Having a staffer who is attending to security and arrangements is so much safer ... I've got a full-time fixer who knows he doesn't want to lose me because it'll be his job, but also who knows, he doesn't want to lose himself. And I'm paying him a salary. Not much, but I'm paying him a salary" (ibid.).

Harm brought about by a local guide is not always intentional, according to Williams. "Many of them were coming at it like 'this is my opportunity to show the outside world what's happening to my people.' And they wanted you to see the full brutality of that. And they weren't thinking, 'I want to put this person in the line of fire.' But because their interests were [not] entirely in sync with my own, you could end up being led someplace [unsafe]. And you never wanted to say to them, 'I don't want to go anywhere that's dangerous' because a whole war-zone is dangerous ... But sometimes, a lot of the time, these people were so inured to the violence going on around them that it didn't occur to them that somebody coming in from the outside who might be more of a target may not be as comfortable" (Williams 2014).

Security Apparatuses versus Blending in

In the early days of the Iraq War ABC News was among the broadcast companies that retained a private security company to accompany its journalists, including newsman Bob Woodruff, enabling them to "wander around Iraq fairly safely." It was a first, for Woodruff. "For the first time in my life, we had actually secured security groups, the Pilgrims Group security team" (Woodruff 2014).

Hiring a security firm is one extra safeguard. Renting armored vehicles is another, which Gutman did once for a "very risky trip into Mostar where we did not have a really good idea of where exactly we were going" (Gutman 2014). Mostar was "being shelled at very close range," and "the Muslim part of the City was under siege ... We were going into the old Muslim part of the town. And we drove down, we drove into no-man's-land several times, getting lost on an airport runway or a road next to an airport and finally giving ourselves up to the Croats" (ibid.).

That night, Gutman and his colleague "slept somewhere in somebody's digs ... Almost the whole town was living in the basement. And when we came out, there was a hole in the glass on the passenger side of the front seat that nearly penetrated three-inch thick glass. So I had a big bill that I had to send my office afterwards for repairing of a window" (ibid.).

That was one of the "hairiest" things Gutman had done, which was not to be repeated. "We decided if I'm going somewhere in an armored car, and Mostar was the big exception, maybe I shouldn't be going there anyway" (ibid.).

Similar to McClatchy, the *Los Angeles Times'* security policy "insisted that we have two cars take a journalist out whenever [one of us was] going to do an interview," according to Williams. But like ABC News, the *Times* also hired armed guards, which Williams argues, may have actually endangered journalists. "They were doing these maneuvers on the highways, so it [would not be] obvious where the foreign journalist was in this convoy, which was ridiculous because it was so obvious because you weren't a normal person just plying the streets. It drew attention to you in a way, I think, which imperils you rather than protects you" (The Scholars' Circle 2012). It was a case of "too much security," which "can be a danger too," Williams argued. "I always kind of have to assess what's the right amount of protection and precaution to take, and what's too much and what's just going to make you a target" (ibid.).

For similar reasons, PC10 avoided colleagues, security, and even using flak jackets. "I think it can make you a target. I've never actually worn a flak jacket," she said (PC10 2014). On one recent assignment in Iraq, she took the gear, "just in case, if I go into a very active frontline, but I never ended up wearing it. My thing is always that I like to try to stay as unnoticeable as possible, blend in as much as possible ... It's so bulky. It's so weird" (ibid.). Unwanted attention is PC10's chief concern. But she also doubts the vest's ability to protect. "Even if you wear the flak jacket, you are covering a very small part of your body ... There's still a lot of ways you could die. And some journalists are just doing daring things ... [and sometimes] it's the luck of the draw because once you go into [say] Aleppo, it's getting barrel bombed" (ibid.).

Gutman did invest in the gear "after journalists started being killed ... We started wearing it as we were traveling through contested zones. But I always felt guilty because I didn't have one for the driver sometimes or for the translator. What am I supposed to do? Carry four sets of heavy gear? You just can't do that. And frankly, did it ever make a difference? Did it ever save my life? No. Most people usually carry it in the boot of the car rather than start in wearing it. But whenever I was going through a contested zone, I felt I owed it to my wife and daughter to put it on" (Gutman 2014).

Protective equipment is cost-prohibitive for many freelance journalists. Jamail, for example, admits that he had "none of that kind of support. No, we were totally on our own" (Jamail 2014). Yet he admits that he "intentionally chose not to" pursue the gear in an effort to remain inconspicuous. "Even if I had access to a helmet or flak jacket I wouldn't have worn it because to me that was almost like being embedded, and I didn't want to do anything that set me aside from Iraqis. I almost felt like my security was in having no security, and that the less I did to draw attention to myself, the more I just kind of blended in" (ibid.).

Blending in was a common strategy among interviewees. Female reporters, for example, wore traditional attire, such as a hijab while in Baghdad and Afghanistan. "At the time, insurgents were kidnapping foreigners and beheading them, [so] I was a little more willing to bow to local tradition. But even just being in the car, you wanted to be covered up so you wouldn't be noticeable," said Williams (2014).

Male reporters also dressed to match the locals, particularly in "a place like Fallujah where I didn't want anyone to know I was a journalist, because people were so paranoid. And the US military was using spies who would often pose as journalists, and the resistance quickly figured this out," said Jamail. "I would just try to go in and act like I was an Iraqi and dress accordingly and let my fixer kind of shepherd me around that way" (Jamail 2014).

When reporting from apartheid South Africa, Parks dressed to be sure he "didn't look like a cop," he said. Blue blazers, he believed, "marked me as a civilian non-combatant ... We had a ritual burning when I left because they were so soaked with tear gas I couldn't give them away" (Parks 2014).

Similar to the two-vehicle rule, the age of mobile telephones-as-tracking-devices has created a two-telephone rule for some regions, such as government-controlled Syria, according to PC10. She carries at least one temporary mobile phone alongside their standard mobile device. The former's SIM card was connected to a false identity, so "it can't be traced back to me" (PC10 2014). Dual phones also protect her sources, as many have been "cut off from any more contact. And as they would say, 'My papers have been burned'" (ibid.).

Pseudonyms and Bylines

John Dinges was already in Chile when General Pinochet and his military forcibly took power from elected President Salvador Allende in 1973. Dinges remained in the country but temporarily stopped reporting. "I'd like to say that I was doing all this clandestine stuff, but I wasn't," he said. "I was sending a little bit of raw information ... but I pretty much had my head down" (Dinges 2014).

Toward the beginning of 1975, however, he "started sticking my head up and ... started working actively as a journalist again." But he used his own name only when writing about non-controversial issues. When covering the Pinochet regime and its human rights abuses for the major US media, such as the *Washington Post* or *Time Magazine*, Dinges rarely sent "anything out with my [byline] on it." And when writing sensitive material for the newsletter *Latin America Press*, he used a pseudonym. "I wrote as Ramon Massamo. He was my guy. I always had great affections for Ramon because it was my editor who invented that name. It gave me the freedom to not worry about what I was doing. The pseudonym gave me protection" (Dinges 2014).

Anonymously or as Ramon Massamo, Dinges did his "most important work, writing about the disappearances," he said. "You're in the middle of a dictatorship. You're figuring out that what the military is doing, that they are not just beating people up and torturing them, but that they're actually hiding their bodies when they kill them. And they're doing this so that the families, the victims' families, are not even able to claim that the government has detained their relative ... And this was a new phenomenon" (ibid.).

A particularly cruel part of the disappearance campaign was called Operation Colombo. In it the regime killed and disappeared people in Chile while publishing lists in magazines claiming that "they were killed in Brazil and Argentina," explained Dinges. "I documented that the people that they said were killed in Brazil and Argentina had actually been disappeared in Chile. And I nailed them on this thing. Open and shut case" (ibid.).

To prevent developing a paper trail on his investigations, Dinges dictated stories over the telephone, phoning information to his Buenos Aires editor at *Time Magazine*. "They were probably tapping the phone, but it was in English so they didn't understand it. I was pretty confident to talk on the phone because ... Of all the people they were tapping, which would be hundreds and hundreds, they would've had to figure out that this particular call … they'd have to have somebody translate it, so I would talk on the phone fairly freely" (ibid.).

Sensitive to the dangers of the Operation Colombo story, *Time*'s Buenos Aires editor suggested Dinges fly to Argentina. "He said, 'Get on a plane and come over to Buenos Aires, and we'll write this story in Buenos Aires.' So I did that and the junta had no idea who wrote that story. Maybe they could've figured it out, but my fingerprints were not on it at all" (ibid.).

Problems emerged only after a new editor arrived at the newsmagazine. "He [my boss] left, and this is a couple of months later. And a new guy comes in who doesn't really understand the situation" (ibid.). Without fully comprehending the political landscape in Chile, the new editor refused to take similar safety measures, despite the concerns that Dinges raised. "When they asked me to [provide documentation], I said, 'Really you should get me out of the country to send this up,' and they said, 'No, just send it by telex'" (ibid.).

It was the rare occasion that Dinges sent sensitive information via telex, instead of either dictating by telephone or flying to Buenos Ares to write stories. "I never transmitted anything by telex like Ramon Massamo or human rights stuff, my main stories that I did on human rights," said Dinges. "But this guy said, 'just send it off,' and I did" (ibid.).

He transmitted twelve disappearance cases across to *Time Magazine*, which Dinges called "a drop in the bucket … I'd been tracking this month by month, so I had all these cases. And I gave them twelve really hot cases, and I did send that by telex … and that was the one they [the Pinochet regime] caught me on" (ibid.).

By late 1976, Dinges had reverted to using his byline in the *Washington Post*, despite warnings from the US Embassy, which cautioned, "You're not going to last very long with that stuff," he recalled. But the risk was important for professional reasons. "I'm writing all these stories, but I have a career to worry about, and I'm not getting any credit for this stuff. And I don't want to stay here forever … This is not just idealism, I'm just trying to, this is careerism. I wanted to get back to the States and have people say, 'Okay, you did good stuff'" (ibid.).

The combined changes landed Dinges into trouble. By mid-February 1977, the Chilean police raided his home and "[came] to the house to arrest me. I didn't know why. I thought it was the secret police, and so I didn't go home for a couple of days, and then I went to the [US] embassy" (ibid.).

By then, the US leadership had changed, with President Jimmy Carter replacing Richard Nixon, which also shifted the political dynamics for Dinges. "The embassy is now suddenly my friend, and a guy from the embassy went with me to the police station. It [was] the PDI [Policía de Investigaciones de Chile/Investigations Police of Chile], the detective agency. They were civilian police, so when I knew that, when I found out it was civilian police, not the secret police, then I was a little bit less worried. And I went in, and the guy was waiting outside, so I knew I wasn't going to disappear" (ibid.).

Dinges was, however, ordered to leave the country. "They read this decree to me ... that I was expelled from the country, and that I had 72 hours to get out" (ibid.). His offense? "'Marxist propaganda, drug trafficking, and/or homosexuality,'" to which Dinges asked, "'Well which one of these?' And they said, 'Well, we don't really know.' I said, 'So I get to choose?' It was pretty funny" (ibid.).

The day before he was set to be expelled, the Chilean government summoned Dinges again, this time to the media control agency where the officer accused him of "purveying propaganda: 'Señor Dinges, we're really worried about the stuff that you've been writing. It's been distorted and blah, blah, blah, and we have the documentation of the erroneous material that you've been [publishing].' He brings out this big file, which are all of my telexes for the past year, back and forth to the *Washington Post* and to *Time Magazine*, which included all my stories. I couldn't get them to give me my file [before then], right?" (ibid.).

In the end, the Chilean government ostensibly gave in to "United States pressure," he said. "Carter was like two weeks in office, so things had changed completely ... DINA [the secret police—Dirección de Inteligencia Nacional/National Intelligence Directorate] wanted to kick me out, and the people around Pinochet wanted to. This was when DINA still existed [and] was running all the terror apparatus" (ibid.). Still, Chilean officials admonished Dinges: "'mend your ways. You've got to learn that you can't do it this way'" (ibid.).

Following the Rules

Following local laws, policies, and customs, particularly entrance visas, can save a journalist's life for two reasons, according to Gutman. First, "I'm not sure whether my insurance company would back up sneaking into a place," and secondly, "Having that piece of paper is something that will get you off the hook at least once on your trip. You're bound to get into trouble when you don't expect it ... On the whole, having those passes makes the difference. It slows the process. It confuses them" (Gutman 2014).

In three separate incidents, the official passes prevented potential disasters for Gutman. In eastern Syria, Gutman and his photographer had gotten unconstrained access to an energy production facility. "Nobody stopped us, and we were permitted. And you try to push your foot as hard as you can on the door," he said. "I had had a very long talk with people at the gas plant, the oil refinery, who told me the whole story of what was going on in the town. And [they] let us have freedom to roam there. We had pictures of the whole plant, things that would get you jailed in five minutes in most war-zones ... We were just wandering, doing things that we thought we could get away with (ibid.).

Gutman knew "we could get in real trouble. And we knew we had to leave town, and I was perfectly willing to do it." But as they exited, a man approached, asking the photographer to take a picture of him, which was noticed by "a guard of the Nusra, which is the Al Qaeda affiliate. And that guy started shouting at Andre [the photographer]. He brought over other people. We got into the deepest shit over it, and we were run out of town. They threatened to take his camera, my computer, everything else ... These were not friendly guys. And you didn't want to get on the wrong side. Also, because they were trigger happy, they were nervous, and they really were worried about themselves, I guess. And in plain clothes, so you didn't know what their ranks were, what their chain of command was. You knew nothing about it" (ibid.).

What rescued them were the "official" visas that Gutman's local guide had obtained and presented. "And the pass, if you can believe it, was from ISIS, from the Islamic State ... They were rivals at that point, and ISIS was trying to take it over but hadn't managed to ... The guys from Nusra looked at the pass and said, 'Ah this is a piece of shit' and took it ... [but] they actually let us leave, and that's why I'm here today ... That pass, they didn't exactly salute. But it did give them pause. So that's all you can do" (ibid.).

During the civil wars of Lebanon, Gutman found himself arrested in the deep south of Lebanon for "something stupid, like I was taking a picture, and the guy was too nearby. And that gets you arrested in many, many places," he said. "You had to carry multiple passes, and you had to know who you were showing it to" (ibid.). Because of Gutman's passes, a soldier "finally brought me to the Israelis, and the Israelis said, 'oh, okay, you're free to go.' But this guy was willing to shoot if necessary. So I think passes are smart. And getting kicked out can happen" (ibid.).

More recently, at the border of Turkey, while Gutman was documenting "civilians desperate to find some shelter," a fuel smuggler seized Gutman and turned him in to the Turkish military. In detention for some nine hours he was restricted from outside communication. But the official passes still provided evidence that he had "not crossed the border illegally ... If I had [crossed illegally], I would have been kicked out of the country" (ibid.).

Despite precautions and careful planning, journalists still find themselves "by accident or by miscalculation ... in a very dodgy place," admitted Gutman (ibid.). During the Bosnian War, for example, he took an official United Nations tour. "I was in an APC [armored personnel carrier] commandeered by the UN with a UN flag on it and escorted by them," he recalled. But when passing through a Serbian-held checkpoint, "the Serbs insisted on seeing a list of who was on board, and they saw my name, and they said, 'We want to talk with this man'" (ibid.). Serb forces pulled Gutman from the vehicle and detained him, and the tour continued on its way. It took hours before Gutman was released. "Some commander or other of the UN force came along and got me freed" (ibid.).

Like Gutman, Parks sought to mind the rules, and most of the time, "we knew what the rules were. We stood on the side, and left when [we] were told to get out. Usually you're okay" (Parks 2014). But still, Parks admits, "I was arrested ten times—for violating emergency regulations" (ibid.).

There were also times when rules and commands were difficult, even impossible to follow—such as during a protest in Capetown, South Africa during the apartheid era: "People were assembling on the playing field of the local teachers' college, in a suburb called Athlone, a 'Colored' suburb. One part was Colored, one part was Asian; that is Indian. And the police had then surrounded the place and were starting then to lob tear gas in. They got the gate locked. Panic. I was rather lighter then, and went over the back wall with a friend, and we go pounding down the street, and the police are gaining on us. We go into a side street and all the houses look the same. They're matchbox houses. Then we see one that's got a bright rainbow painted on it. 'Oh, that looks interesting.' We pounded on the front door. Nobody comes. Then we run round to the back. There are a couple of people sitting out there. And I'm dripping sweat, [in my] blue blazer. And they just took us in and gave us wet towels to wipe our face. The house belongs to a very accomplished musician, Dower Brand, formerly known as Abdullah Ibraham. I spent the day in Dower Brand's house" (ibid.).

In another incident, the police "with shot guns and these big whips" chased the journalists down a main street. "I go running as fast as I could, and there are two guys standing in the doorway of a butcher's shop, a halal butcher's shop. And they said, 'Come on in.' They put me in the meat locker until all the stuff had passed," recalled Parks, adding that the police injured *The London Times* reporter. "The guy I was running with kept on running ... and he got a back full of bird shot—whole back."

Similarly, while covering Southern Lebanon, Parks and a Reuters journalist drove a Volkswagen Beetle through PLO [Palestine Liberation Organization] lines for an interview where a soldier was "pretty unhappy to see us, like, 'how did you get here?'" Parks recalled. "[While] we were driving back, and we were zipping along and all of a sudden, we hear gun shots behind us. Well, that moment, you've got to make a choice. In a VW, you back up ... So we backed up, talked to this PLO guy, and managed to get the right laissez-passer [visa] out of the right pocket. And then he got on his radio and told the next guys to let us through" (ibid.).

Training

The growing adversities have given birth to an industry that trains and prepares danger zone journalists for the field, simulating worst case scenarios such as abductions, ambushes, and medical emergencies as part of the training. Large media organizations usually fund the training for staff reporters (Tenore 2012), and some, such as ABC News in the US, have made the training mandatory for foreign correspondents. "At ABC we had a very strict rule that we did have to get some training before I went over there," said Woodruff (2014).

The development was applauded by veteran journalists such as Gutman. "There [are] now three or four [companies] that train you in dealing with hostile environments. And I personally have great support for those guys because they just simply heighten your awareness of what can happen and what to do [in those situations]" (Gutman 2014).

Gutman believes that the training could have prevented some of the casualties among his peers, including Daniel Pearl who was kidnapped and beheaded in 2002 by Pakistani militants. "He never went through the hostile environments training because the *Wall Street Journal* didn't do that sort of thing then, which would have given him some awareness of what to do in dangerous areas," Gutman said (ibid.).

The risk itself is something Gutman says he, too, "might have taken." But he argued, "I would've had a backup. And I also would have thought twice about who these guys are … Pearl stumbled into a trap. They were looking for a case. It may have just been bad luck as well. But there were some precautions that could've been taken" (ibid.).

While at Reuters, Schlesinger said he advocated for more training before journalists left for the field so correspondents could protect themselves, respond appropriately to gunfire and learn basic first aid (Schlesinger 2014). Reuters also sought to pair up new correspondents with more experienced staff "to transmit that knowledge through the organization" and to make available experienced support staff "at headquarters" who "can be that sounding board at any hour of the day or night" (ibid.).

Lifesaving first aid has become a key component in the hostile environment training, also arising from the growing injuries sustained by correspondents. Historically, journalists have had "no idea how to save someone's life," said Woodruff. Now, it has become more common for journalists to learn basic medical treatment. "Journalists are more open to be trained for that because the reality has changed" (Woodruff 2014).

The Trouble with Freelance

Economic pressures on for-profit news organizations have led to closed bureaus, reduced foreign reporting budgets and personnel, spurring a greater reliance on freelance journalists for danger zone coverage. "There are more people freelancing, taking risks. So let me say a couple of things about freelancers. Some of them do incredibly brave things. Some do incredibly stupid things," remarked Parks, adding that unlike staff correspondents, "he or she doesn't know the audience as well" (Parks 2014).

The greatest challenge for freelance journalists or stringers are resources, he explained. "They don't have the resources, and resources matter. When Alissa Rubin got hurt in Iraq, [for example], she was back in Paris 48 hours later being taken care of. Nobody's looking after those [freelance] guys who get picked up. Terry Anderson, when he was collected and held for years, was a cause. When Hamas held a BBC correspondent in Gaza, he was a cause. He was important to his colleagues. You have no colleagues as a freelancer. Lastly, you don't have someone on the other end of the phone saying, 'no' [when it's too dangerous]" (ibid.).

Growing hostilities have diminished the help that freelancers traditionally received from journalists on staff at large media organizations, according to McCarthy, who had relied upon "the generosity and assistance of more seasoned colleagues" when he began his journalism career. "People still do [that], but there are limits, and I remember a number of times when I've been approached by freelancers in Kabul or Baghdad, and I'd say, 'I'd love to help you, but we're not going to get this cleared by our bosses. They'll say, well, here's another person. Have they had their security training? Are they insured? Have they got medical insurance, got medevac?' Well, probably not" (McCarthy 2014).

Nor can freelancers afford full-time local guides in the ways that large media companies can, forcing them to frequently "rely on the kindness of strangers," according to Gutman (2014).

As a freelance journalist, Stephenson knows the predicament firsthand. He found himself "getting by on next to nothing and being forced to take risks as a result of that, that I wouldn't otherwise choose to take, not [just] to get the stories, but just to be there, staying in a less secure place than I might otherwise choose to stay just because that's a function of money," he said. "That's just one example. Not being able to afford a translator, a full-time translator or a fixer. It's just so expensive. [Some correspondents] have whole teams of them ... I've driven into Iraq and out of Iraq at times when, if I'd had a choice, I would've flown because it's just so much safer, but I just didn't have the money to spend on the very expensive flights" (Stephenson 2014).

Some freelancers have managed to obtain training, equipment, and other safety products. Szlanko for example, frequently travels with safety equipment. He has taken the hostile environment training, including "two medical trainings, first aid training," he said (Szlanko 2014).

But other freelance journalists have had less opportunity. It's only one additional complication for the stringers in a changing profession. A series of nonprofit organizations have emerged to support freelance danger zone journalists. One of them, RISC (Reporters Instructed in Saving Colleagues), was founded by journalist, author, and filmmaker Sebastian Junger after his colleague Tim Hetherington died in the field from a war-related injury, a death that Junger believed might have been prevented, had the journalists been properly trained.

Embedding and Safety

Journalists have long made choices about covering conflicts either unilaterally or while embedded with a military. But as conflicts have descended into the worst violence, correspondents have been left with fewer safe options. Embedding with militaries, however, does not guarantee safety, as interviews demonstrated. "In Iraq I came in unilateral, which meant driving after the troops in our own car from Kuwait, and we very nearly got killed then. In Afghanistan, I was embedded and very nearly got killed then. So I'm not sure what is more safe. You're in a war-zone," explained McCarthy (The Scholars' Circle 2012).

Woodruff was embedded with the US 4th infantry division when he fell victim to an improvised explosive device (IED). Despite wearing body armor and helmets, the attack severely injured him and his colleague, Canadian cameraman Doug Vogt. Woodruff's brain injury caused a year-long struggle with aphasia. But one advantage to embedding, Woodruff noted, is the medical care. "These guys are incredibly well-trained, I was embedded when I was badly hit. If I didn't have someone trained, like they had, to stop that bleeding in me, I would not be alive right now. I could have gotten hit by an IED easily if I was just out there with one of my ABC crews. If I was, I would not be alive because I don't think there's any chance in hell they would have been able to stop that bleeding ... I can't even say that for sure, but I just think that the best one they could have found was those guys, the military, the ones that were the people around me that stopped the bleeding, rushed me off by helicopter to stabilize me. They thought I was going to be dead anyway, so without someone that advanced, I wouldn't be alive right now" (Woodruff 2014).

Woodruff also believes that relationships between military and journalists may "have changed," since the Vietnam War. "I think there was such a massive division between media and the military, and I think that has shrunk down significantly now because back then nobody wanted to talk to each other. So now we do talk to each other" (ibid.).

Most interviewed foreign correspondents had reported both unilaterally and embedded with militaries. Some had embedded with both state militaries and with rebel groups, such as Kurdish and Syrian rebel fighters. While embedding has offered some protection, medical care, and greater access to some aspects of conflicts, they acknowledge that it has simultaneously compromised aspects of their work in preventing the so-called "first casualty" of war—the truth—discussed in Chapter 6 titled, "The First Casualty."

New Media Dangers

New media have created new dangers—for both foreign and local danger zone journalists. And while "the internet has been a fantastic democratizing force," empowering "people who have never had it before by giving them access to a worldwide audience," it "equally lends itself to malign purpose. And I think it's pretty clear it's put power in the hands of people who want to kill. So that's a new kind of obstacle that's been put in the way of independent journalists and independent journalism," explained Allan Little (2015).

Dictators use the web and social networks to identify dissidents; narcotraffickers use them to track critics and opponents, including journalists. "Journalists are now facing friends who are in their Facebook, in their social media [who] now, they're part of the narco-trafficking," explained Claudia Nunez to the Los Angeles Press Club. "It's a war even in the social media with the Mexican journalists ... There's no protection. If people go and click and make some comments, now they are the targets of the narco-trafficking ... These people are involved in technology, big business, people who know how to track information" (The Scholars' Circle 2012).

These problems persist for local danger zone journalists but have a different quality to them. Local journalists who live in the danger zones must contend with the dangers with fewer safety options and on a daily basis. Their backstories about their stories follow in Chapter 5, "Living in a Danger Zone."

References

Dinges, John. 2014. Personal Interview. In Person. Washington, DC. November 3.

Glazer, Andrew. 2014. Personal Interview. In Person. Brooklyn, NY. October 31.

Gold, Danny. 2014. Personal Interview. In Person. Brooklyn, NY. October 31.

Gutman, Roy. 2014. Personal Interview. Via Skype. Auckland to Istanbul. December 6.

Helsinki Watch. 1992. "War Crimes in Bosnia-Hercegovina." Report by Human Rights Watch. https://www.hrw.org/reports/pdfs/y/yugoslav/yugo.928/yugo928 full.pdf#page=1&zoom=auto,-150,217. Accessed March 26, 2016.

Jamail, Dahr. 2014. Personal Interview. Via Telephone. November 10.

Little, Allan. 2015. Personal Interview. Via Telephone. Auckland to London. January 27.

McCarthy, Terry. 2014. Personal Interview. In Person. Los Angeles. July 7.

Mojica, Jason. 2014. Personal Interview. In Person. Brooklyn, NY. October 31.

Parks, Michael. 2014. Personal Interview. Los Angeles. November 18.

PC10. 2014. Personal Interview. In Person. Site withheld. November 11.

PJ09. 2014. Personal Interview. In Person. Site withheld. November 10.

Schlesinger, David. 2014. Personal Interview. Via Skype. Aukland to Hong Kong. November 27.

The Scholars' Circle. 2012. "Reporting from the Danger Zone." Panel Discussion. First broadcast September 30, 2012.

Stephenson, Jon. 2014. Personal Interview. In Person. Auckland, NZ. December 12.

Szlanko, Balint. 2014. Personal Interview. Via Skype. November 12.

Tenore, Mallory Jean. 2012. "How Journalists Train to Stay Safe while Covering Hostile Environments." *Poynter. A Global Leader in Journalism.* April 11. http://www.poynter.org/news/mediawire/169264/how-journalists-train-to-cover-hostile-environments/. Accessed December 29, 2012.

Williams, Carol. 2014. Personal Interview. In Person. Los Angeles. June 26.

Woodruff, Bob. 2014. Personal Interview. Via Telephone. Los Angeles to New York. November 13.

5 Living in a Danger Zone

Unfathomable

"I can't believe what's happening to my country." It was a common sentiment among interviewed local and dual-identity danger zone journalists (Interviews 2014).

In Bosnia, Kemal Kurspahic, editor of the daily Sarajevo newspaper, *Oslobodjenje* (Liberation), could hardly fathom the siege arriving at his doorstep. Nor did he anticipate the scale of the human calamity. After World War II, the former Yugoslavia embraced Josip Broz Tito's slogan of "brotherhood and unity," he said. "We were raised in that internationalist spirit, and had some expectations from the international community that someone would do something early in the siege" when it "wouldn't take a whole army or full-scale intervention" (Kurspahic 2014).

Also unimaginable was the civilian toll, which Kurspahic still vividly remembers two decades later. "I can see the blasts coming from the tank at the top, next to the monument at the top of the hill and hitting neighboring high-rise buildings and setting fire to [them]. I had two apartment buildings burn completely, just 200 meters from where I live, and they were 21-floor high apartment buildings. So when that whole thing is burning, it became so hot, even [for] those a few hundred meters away in my apartment, it was unbearably hot. And that night, in one of those buildings, [where] I think 700 people lived, and [I remember] seeing them, sobbing, taking their plastic bags with nothing left. And those were all Bosnians, Serbs, Muslims, Croats. There was no one spared. It was a Serb siege, but Serbs suffered too" (ibid.).

For years, Kurspahic and his colleagues had been fighting for media freedom, protesting a new legal effort to place media under control of the Parliament. Nearly 5,000 people had come out in the streets to demonstrate before Kurspahic and his colleagues mounted a legal challenge in the constitutional court (ibid.).

By a narrow margin, they won the case: The court overturned the Act, which had required the media to answer to government-appointed executives (ibid.).

"And then the war erupted."

Destruction was widespread, affecting every aspect of life, making conditions arduous and grim. "The siege lasted three and a half years, and for long periods of time, there was no electricity; there was no heat. You live in [a] windowless apartment in [the] Olympic city, [the] winter Olympic city with freezing temperatures, and life is miserable," recalled Kurspahic. "Some of your family or whole family was gone to some safer place. Serbs and Croats had that option to leave the city because there were checkpoints, and you use your ID [to get] through checkpoints" (ibid.).

Not so for Bosniaks, the Bosnians of the Muslim faith. Nor for Serbs or Croats who "collaborated" with Bosniaks (ibid.).

Bleak conditions were compounded by the dangers that journalists faced. Snipers shot at them; nationalist forces publicly ridiculed them, eliminated their jobs; and many lost friends and relatives in the war. Kurspahic worked amidst "artillery positions, sniper positions, machine guns, 200 meters away with nothing in between [them and us], point blank ... We were on the frontline," he said. "The siege started in April '92. Sometime early in the siege, maybe end of May, early June, first my office was sprayed by machine gun [fire], and all the windows gone ... We were all exposed to the same terror of the siege" (ibid.).

While most of Yugoslavia divided along ethnic lines, the *Oslobodjenje* staff remained ethnically diverse, according to Kurspahic: Serb journalists, such as Branko Tomic, worked alongside Kurspahic, who is Bosniak until a Serb television station publicly accused Tomic of working with the "enemy." "They ran a story [about] Serbs working for ... [the] president of Bosnia, and they mentioned their names, saying 'Serbians [were] feeding their families [while] they work for that "Muslim" paper,'" he said. "We helped Branko's wife and kids, who lived with her parents in Serbia, to escape, first to Macedonia, then to Sweden. Then Branko joined them later in '94. So there was this issue of your family's safety" (ibid.).

Despite risks and harsh conditions, Kurspahic and his colleagues couldn't quit "for at least three reasons," he said. "One is the tradition of the paper that started as [a] liberation movement paper in [the] Second World War in [the] Bosnian mountains in '43. So we have that tradition. [Secondly], we had a newly found respect among our readership, being the main paper fighting for independence, taking a strong position, so we owe it to our readers, and [thirdly], we owe it to our profession. There were dozens of foreign journalists coming to cover what's called 'the war' here ... So even when those things happened—people getting hurt, some killed ... I never doubted whether we should or shouldn't [keep reporting]" (ibid.).

Residents of Sarajevo also relied on the daily paper for basic information—such as "whether there will be another round of humanitarian aid distribution," or if their loved ones were injured or had died. This vital information complemented daily reports about the war's development (ibid.).

But the job was perilous. One *Oslobodjenje* photographer stopped to photograph a water queue because "we didn't have running water in our apartments. So the people are waiting to just get some basic canisters of water," recalled Kurspahic. "He stopped and took a picture, and another mortar shell exploded, killing three people in the line, and it killed him. He was only identified by his camera" (ibid.).

As Serb forces crossed into Bosnia, another reporter covering the "imminent fall of Zvornik" joined the fallen. "He [had] sent his family out on a truck with refugees fleeing the town. The town was shelled for two or three days from the other side of the river. And [on] the day they entered the town, he talked with our regional office secretary in the town of Tuzla, and sent her some scribbled notes on where the shelling is coming from. He identified a few places in town being shelled and so on, and he said, 'Quickly, send this to Sarajevo. I hear their steps. They're coming for me'" (ibid.).

For two weeks, the editorial team heard nothing more from him. "Then his son called me from exile as [a] refugee," recalled Kurspahic. "[He] said, 'Uncle Kemal, my father [has been] killed.' And I said, 'Wait, maybe not, people got caught, arrested, detained, you might hear.' 'No,' he said, 'We talked with two people who saw him dead. One neighbor who saw him being dragged by legs out of the office, dead,' He said, 'like an animal. The woman told me' ... He knew he was facing a death threat, and he stayed reporting until he died" (ibid.).

These personal losses profoundly anguished local journalists. "There is a huge difference [for local journalists], because if your city is under terror, those are all your friends, your family, your relatives, people you care about. You care about all the people. I can care about anyone experiencing suffering, but those are your neighbors, people you know," explained Kurspahic. "I open my obituary page in my paper, and every morning I see the faces of people killed yesterday that I met [with] two days ago. There is my colleague from Bosnian Radio, Zeljko Ruzicic, who was killed. I met [with] him a few days before he was killed. He was collecting some documents, some papers to go to, I think, Australia to do some kind of reporting, all from [the] Bosnian diaspora there. And Drago [had] asked me, he said, 'We [will] have to see what you need from me while I'm there. What can I do for you?' And he was killed in the center of the city by a shell that exploded near the Bosnian presidency building. And [I] was very close when that explosion happened. I was in a street facing that part of the town, and there was a horrifying sound of an explosion, and the air coming with it because it was a narrow street, and you could feel the wind. And only later, I saw his picture in the obituaries, and only later I connected that was that moment when Drago was killed" (ibid.).

Friendship betrayals were another occupational hazard. "In order to get their new base and get some job or something, a few of them decided to say that *Oslobodjenje* became [a] 'Muslim paper' headed by 'Muslim fundamentalist'—me," recalled Kurspahic. Some betrayals were life-threatening. "One of my staff members [to] whom I gave [his] first job, [his] brother [was] in [the] Serb unit, targeting my paper ... Two ten-floor high twin [buildings], one flat part of the building where my offices were, it was just my windows gone. And they also hit a painting that was on the wall just behind where I sit. And if I were there, it would [have] killed me" (ibid.).

The violence, the chaos and the shortages required hypervigilance, split-second adjustments, and resourcefulness. After Serb forces shelled *Oslobodjenje*'s offices, for example, Kurspahic and the rest of the staff bifurcated their operations into two locations—"[an] atomic bomb shelter underneath" the old building and a set of "offices in the part of the city next to the presidency building, so we could report from the city" (ibid.).

When power and communication lines were cut, they retrenched to more primitive operations. "We didn't have telephone; we didn't have fax, we didn't have electricity," said Kurspahic. "Everyone would type their stories on old fashioned typewriters, and one of the reporters would collect all the stories, all the photos, films, negatives that day and bring it from the downtown to the paper's building" (ibid.).

Delivery was another high-risk job. Gunmen stalked the route between the rented offices and the newspaper's old building. "That was that sniper area. You had to go down that sniper area for about, I think, six kilometers from the town center to the paper's building. And there were some people shot at while doing that part of the job," recalled Kurspahic.

To minimize exposure, staff rotated in seven-day shifts, remaining inside the bomb shelter for seven days and nights in a row. "I would have a team of essential editors come in Mondays and stay until the next Monday, seven days, sleeping there, eating, whatever we could provide, and making sure the paper is done, prepared every day. And then the next Monday there would be another shift, up to ten people, including a few printing workers" (ibid.).

Fuel shortages troubled production and distribution, which required some 100 liters of diesel per day. But without a working gas station in the entire city and a black market where prices climbed to $20–25 per liter, Kurspahic and his team secured a 20-day supply (2,000 liters) of fuel from the then Commander General in the United Nations. By going to the top of the UN, Kurspahic and his team could circumvent the black market, "which had to be supplied by someone in the UN" (ibid.).

Family trauma, stress, and grief compounded professional troubles. After a car accident injured Kurspahic, he organized to transport his family to safer ground in Croatia, via the United Nations. But separation anxieties affected his children. "[The] last day of October, I had them all boarding that plane, and my younger son was crying and begging me, 'Dad, will you bring me back?' ... because there was also that sense of solidarity amongst kids, neighboring kids. They were so together through [so much]. He was only 11, and he didn't want us to leave" (ibid.).

With his family on safer ground and his injury treated, Kurspahic returned to work in Sarajevo. But "I couldn't keep in touch on any basis. There was no telephone line. Occasionally you can use a satellite telephone; I had one in the office, but I never used it for personal calls because I couldn't afford letting others use it, and [so] I just couldn't use it myself. So there was no communication, and [my wife] knew that I was in a shooting zone on crutches in a place where everyone runs across the street for their life," he explained. "I think my wife might be right to some extent in blaming me as not being a good father or husband ... I think she might have a point that I didn't have time to think of things personal ... So I can understand, to some extent" (ibid.).

Despite the shelling of their offices, targeted killings of journalists, and the daily hardships of simply staying alive, Bosnian journalists published *Oslobodjenje* "without missing a day," according to Kurspahic. "I don't think anyone has published a paper under conditions like we did for three and a half years" (ibid.).

Kurspahic is probably correct in his assessment. The journalists' ordeal in Bosnia was extraordinary. At the same time that wars raged in the former Yugoslavia, another European war had been simmering for two decades—the "long war" for the six counties of Ireland, or Northern Ireland. It was a time and place when journalists were much less likely to be targeted for bodily harm. But they still faced another set of difficulties. And like Kurspahic, they shared a deep emotional connection to their community, which guided their stories.

Reporting a Long War in Northern Ireland

How could they justify the assassination? That's what journalists Eamonn Mallie and Brian Rowan wanted to know. But to get the answers, they had to meet the paramilitary group's agents at a secret spot. When they arrived at the remote location, the journalists were blindfolded, seated in a vehicle and driven to another clandestine building. There, they could remove blindfolds and black tape. Standing before them were two Irish Republican Army (IRA) men, faces hidden under balaclavas, who handed them a long sheet of toilet paper that contained the IRA's statement, justifying the latest slaying. The chosen medium, toilet paper, allowed reporters to flush the statements down toilets if raided by police. Statements in hand, the reporters were re-blindfolded and driven back to their original locations. Mallie swallowed the statement but informed his sources it was the last time he would wear a blindfold (Mallie 2009, 2010).

Another local journalist accompanied a former member of the disbanded Official IRA to "stand trial" before a panel of provisional[1] republicans who would dictate his fate. The former IRA man had opposed the new IRA's activities and positions. "I wrote a story about this guy and how he was entrapped ... We had to arrange for him to be brought before the republican movement" where the man "essentially pleaded for his life ... I sat at one side; he sat at the top; there was a crucifix on the wall," he recalled. "And we negotiated this man's survival, basically ... He was told that he can leave, but he can never come back, not even for a funeral for his father or mother ... This man was looked upon as a pariah because he had betrayed, as they perceived, the community. Betrayed the movement, as they saw it" (McLaughlin 2009).

These incidents and the atmosphere of the region generated uneasiness among journalists who covered the Northern Ireland conflict. "I lived a life for many years where you were almost afraid to talk to yourself because of who [else] you were talking to," said one reporter. "It impacted not just on me but on my entire family. There were moments when I feared for my life, feared for my family, feared for everything ... but I got out the other end of this" (IJ2 2009).[2]

Mallie also found it "dangerous for some journalists. By God, it was dangerous," he said. "My whole family was living in fear" (Mallie 2009).

Despite fears and dangers of reporting conflict, in the battle for Northern Ireland, unlike Bosnia or twenty-first century wars, journalists were rarely targets. "If you're a war correspondent, you're in some danger. But we have been low risk," explained journalist and author David McKittrick. "Only one journalist has been killed out of 3,700 deaths" (McKittrick 2009).

It was a different time and place for journalism. Some protected journalists from physical harm, but others believed that journalists were courted as part of the war strategy, particularly by the IRA. The IRA "weren't really going after journalists," said one. "Although in the 1970s, the IRA beat some journalist(s) up, [the republicans] were trying to court journalists and the media ... The Seinners [sic] and the IRA are [were] more under control," referring to the degree of discipline and coordination within the IRA and its army council. That wasn't necessarily true of other paramilitary organizations, he said. The loyalist paramilitary groups were "much more dangerous" and more inclined to "go after" journalists (IJ1 2009).

For some, their fears were rooted in their early life experiences living in the conflict zone. Mallie recalled growing up with a consistent sense of dread. As a Catholic boy in an overtly anti-Catholic region, "I was terrified. I was terrified of loyalism and the Orange Order," he admitted. "It was a menacing time. Where we lived, we got corralled on the Twelfth of July. It was the Orange marches. They come right around and thump these big drums and put the fear of God into you. I would have been afraid of these people ... Even to this day, I have nightmares. I wake up in a sweat. Even last week, when I woke up, I was begging someone not to hang me" (Mallie 2009, 2010).

Other journalists faced similar threats connected to their ethnicity or religion. "Our house was petrol bombed," recalled another journalist. "It was because we were Catholic ... And I knew who did it" (IJ1 2009).

Mostly, journalists resisted revealing these emotional factors in their work, concealing the death threats that they received, while they continued reporting and ensuring security for themselves and their families. And unlike foreign correspondents, they remained in the danger zone throughout their days and nights. "This is not like a correspondent being sent to another zone to report a war and then to leave there after several months to come home. I lived here," remarked an interviewee (IJ2 2009).

Another threat for local Northern Ireland journalists was to their livelihoods, which required a delicate dance of objectivity, as political leaders sized them up for their ideologies and ethnic or religious identities. While foreign correspondents flew into the region with freedom to report as they desired, local journalists faced professional hurdles. "People wanted to figure out if you are on their side or not ... If you came from the Catholic side, you were perceived to be nationalist, and if you came from the Protestant side, you were perceived to be unionist," said IJ7 (2010).

Interviewees had "been discriminated against. I suffered in my business. I nearly went bankrupt," said one journalist (McLaughlin 2009).

Fear about damaging professional reputations or losing access to sources created tacit boundaries around questions journalists could ask, subjects they could pursue, and language they could use, with the deleterious effect of silencing journalists on important topics. For example, when a gunman had shot dead human rights lawyer Pat Finucane in his home while he dined with his family, journalists wanted to investigate the allegation of collusion between loyalist paramilitary groups and British agents, "who at least let it happen," said IJ7. The collusion "has now been established [by the Stevens Report]. There was collusion [between the British agents and the loyalists] in that case." But local journalists were constrained by their identities: "If you lived here and you asked very legitimate questions about the collusion, and you were from a Catholic/nationalist family, then automatically, it was 'oh you've got an agenda here'. But it was a very reasonable question" (IJ7 2010).

Language was also a barrier, said IJ7. "It was hard to choose language when interviewing people. They can't even get agreement about what to call the second largest city. Was it Derry, or was it Londonderry? So if you interview a unionist politician and [call it] 'Derry,' you're automatically [suspect]. You have to alter your language so you don't offend" (ibid.).

Although on the surface, the dispute over a city name may seem trivial, it symbolized legitimacy and belonging. "Derry," for example, connoted that the six-county region legitimately belonged to the Republic of Ireland and should be free of British rule while "Londonderry" meant that the region was still legitimately part of Great Britain (Journalist interviews 2009, 2010).

Similarly, while "the unionist politicians and the government called the IRA 'terrorists,' if you were a reporter, and you typed up the word 'terrorist,' there goes your Sinn Fein contact," said IJ7. Eventually, the media and parties to the conflict agreed to call them and the loyalist fighters "paramilitaries," which IJ7 argued was "not even the right term for these people. But that's what they ended up being called as a 'neutral' term" (IJ7 2010).

While "objectivity" helped shield journalists from accusations of bias, it was their humanitarian values that guided their stories. As explained by one BBC reporter in a conference paper, "With deep roots in the community, some [journalists] lost close relatives ... Can you really, one wonders, be an impartial fly on the wall when the society in which you live is being torn apart from within?"

Probably not, most interviewees admitted, at least not while their community was being torn asunder and while friends were being killed. "Journalists who live in this society covered this process. We covered the conflict, and we had it up to the back teeth with attending funerals and [hearing] the vicious cycle of 'he-said-she-said,'" remarked IJ7 (2010). Added another, "We were sick of reporting murder, destruction, and death. We were sick of it, the senseless killing of people, children" (IJ1 2009).

Eamonn Mallie "hated the violence," which motivated him to better understand its causes. "I'll tell you what that did for me. It decided for me to take risks ... It spurred me on to be more inquisitive and to try to understand why the IRA [was] doing what it was doing, why the UVF[3] was doing what it was doing, why the UDA[4] was doing what it was doing. I kept pushing the envelope and frontiers. A manifestation of that was when I sought permission in various channels within republicanism and loyalism ... to gain access to the Maze prison to try to speak with the IRA and UVF to get explanations of why the IRA were involved in what was then the H-Block and why the UVF were wrecking the cells. So even though I vehemently opposed the IRA campaign of violence and the loyalist campaign of violence, there was deep curiosity in me. I had no empathy or sympathy with [the paramilitaries], but I wanted to understand why did A equals B equals C" (Mallie 2009, 2010).

Mallie lambasted "that campaign of violence that the IRA carried on ... ceaselessly and endlessly." And he acknowledged that he was "preoccupied with the preservation of life" and worried about developing a "Nazi complex ... because of what the IRA were doing ... I genuinely feared that I would end up with a complex like what the Nazis had done to the Jews" (ibid.).

He recalled "a terrible bombing in Ballygally ... The poor soldiers were killed in a bus going to Enniskillen. When the bomb went off, some of them actually crawled across the road, down into an old farm yard, and one or two of them died behind bales of straw." After the incident, he publicly challenged Sinn Fein leader Gerry Adams "about the morality of violence, which resulted in human beings dying behind bales of hay and straw" (ibid.).

Mallie also interviewed Bobby Sands, the republican who won a parliamentary election while on a hunger strike in jail. But rather than sharing in what appeared to be international sympathy for Sands's plight, he expressed fury about Sands's justification for violence. "I had gone to the scene of Earl Mountbatten's killing ... I had also covered the Narrow Water bombing outside Newry, when 18 soldiers were killed ... I had covered both. And I was furious with him. I'll tell you why I was furious with him. He justified the killing of an 80-year-old man on a boat with his family. I couldn't subscribe to that, you know" (ibid.).

Many interviewees expressed what editor and broadcaster Martin McGinley called "trouble fatigue" from the humanitarian toll of violence. "Reporters are from the community, so we were all affected ... Every Monday, I had to go out and talk with someone who lost her husband," he said. On one assignment, he spoke with "five bereaved families in one morning. You don't want to see that going on ... We were traumatized" (McGinley 2009, 2010).

Another editor "used to hate Friday mornings because the IRA would invariably choose a target around mid-morning on a Friday because they knew it would get on the one o'clock news, the lunchtime news. I remember one Friday morning when I passed a butcher shop, and I remember a man called John Smith being shot dead. He was a part-time UDR [Ulster Defence Regiment] soldier. His full-time occupation was a laborer. He was the only son of a widow. For some reason, that has always struck me, that we have ... an ordinary name doing a mundane job, being shot, a calculated shot at a certain time in the morning ... Not every killing happened like that, but invariably, it happened at the end of the week to maximize publicity ... The papers would then do the story full up for Saturday morning. Then that story would be taken on by the Sunday papers, and then the funeral would happen on a Monday" (McLaughlin 2009).

Years or lifetimes in the conflict zone formulated local journalists' judgments about the conflict and the warring parties, shaping their stories. Most interviewees favored peacemakers over fighters, and they recognized the latter's complexity and evolution. "When the Canary Wharf [bomb] happened, [Gerry Adams][5] seemed shattered," said Mallie. "I think as those guys grew older, I think increasingly that sense of religion and being a Catholic ... about not killing and all of that and the repentance and the penance ... had an influence on them ... I remember talking with [Martin] McGuinness[6] eleven or twelve days before the ceasefire. I had a very open discussion with him. I said, 'I want to say something to you;

I cannot personally justify or tolerate the taking of life and being a Catholic. They're incompatible in my world.' Do you know what he said to me? [He said], 'How do you think I feel?' And he had been ... one of the big marksmen" (Mallie 2009, 2010).

Their evolution was most noticeable during the peace process. "Journalists saw these people up close, and they saw the change in them," remarked IJ7. "[We] saw that these people genuinely wanted to make peace," which "sparked changes" in reporting (IJ7 2010).

Interviewees also criticized the establishment parties as "stuck, like the pre-Mandela South Africa ... They were saying, 'we have something, and we're holding onto it; but we're not holding onto it in a very fair way' ... [They] didn't like or want the peace process. They wanted it to stop. Looking back, it looks like they were wrong to do that," said McKittrick. "The [Ulster] Unionist Party back then was saying each year, 'oh, it's getting a little bit better; it will be okay. And this is as good as it gets,'" but they "lost the intellectual argument by saying, 'Just keep a steady ship'. But everybody looked around and said, 'well, this isn't much of a ship; it's just a recipe for violence. The violence is going down a little in statistical terms, but not the capacity for violence; and it's broken; it's not working. We need to do something'" (McKittrick 2009).

As the peace process began to take shape, journalists' hopes for peace shaped their stories. "There might be the odd, crazy journalist who liked reporting on those things, but certainly, everybody was for peace. We're war correspondents but we're also citizens ... People were dying. This is coffins, this is funerals. These are human beings," acknowledged McKittrick (ibid.).

Still, two interviewees believed their colleagues' enthusiasm for a peace agreement prevented proper scrutiny of a flawed process and agreement. "That bias, [the] de facto [desire for peace] was there throughout ... and overruled everything ... anything you could do to get peace, even in the short term," recalled Eamonn McCann. "I remember a political correspondent at the *Irish Times* who ... around 1980 wouldn't cover the Sinn Fein conference on the grounds that 'I will not dignify them by ... pretending that they are a normal party.' They wouldn't do it. A little later, only 14 years, and you aren't allowed to criticize them [Sinn Fein]" (McCann 2009).

Local journalists also faced government restrictions—an official broadcast ban that forbade them from "talking to terrorists" and informal shunning—in place on the grounds that, "you're encouraging them. You're promoting the war ... The big theme, journalistically, overall and politically was, 'You don't talk with the men of terror, the men of violence,'" explained McKittrick (2009).

McKittrick was one of the journalists who "talked to as many terrorists as you could find, really ... Thatcher frowned on that ... [but] we'd be in touch with republicans or IRA messengers all the time. It was part of what the media did ... We had to go to the IRA and say, 'Why did you do that? You killed civilians.' So all the journalists knew IRA people, [and] all the journalists knew how to get in touch with the IRA ... Sometimes, you'd get an interview or a briefing or whatever, but usually, you didn't get much of an answer back from them" (ibid.).

Broadcasters circumvented the official ban either by paraphrasing the banned leaders' statements or by lip-syncing their words with precision. "There was a lot of controversy about this solution that the BBC came up with ... to give some voice to Sinn Fein ... so we lip-synced," said McGinley who worked at the BBC at the time (McGinley 2009, 2010).

Journalism was for some a means of confronting society's ills. Eamonn McCann, for example, acknowledged campaigning for civil rights, human rights, trade unionism and socialism while also reporting on related developments. "I decided that I shouldn't hide the fact that I have strong opinions ... for social justice and for legal rights. I don't pretend to be an objective reporter ... And what's more, I don't believe that any of the others are either" (McCann 2009). Another interviewee used journalism to "keep an eye on things" in the region or to achieve "closure" on past injustices for aggrieved persons (IJ1 2009).

Conditions for journalists in Bosnia and Northern Ireland contrasted with circumstances in Pakistan, Mexico, Liberia, and Russia. But interviewees from all of these countries shared a deep desire to contribute to their communities and improve their countries. Each situation was rife with its own complications. In Pakistan, the most dangerous country for journalists in 2014,[7] violence against journalists is rampant and perpetrated with impunity. Since 1992, at least 75 journalists have been killed, according to the Committee to Protect Journalists, and in the 14 years between 2001 and 2015, The Pakistan Press Foundation counted 384 incidents of violence against journalists—with only two convictions (Pakistani Press Foundation 2015). The crisis state has developed into a new normal, according to award-winning journalist, Umar Cheema. His story is next.

Reporting in Pakistan

"Normalcy is a relative term," said Umar Cheema about working as an investigative journalist in Pakistan. Cheema got a bitter taste of that danger when he reported on a sensitive, off-limits topic—the Pakistani intelligence agency (Cheema 2015).

It was an otherwise unremarkable evening. After dinner with friends, Cheema climbed into his car for a normally easy drive home. But his drive was cut short. A group of men in commando fatigues and "no fear" emblazoned on their shirts forced Cheema to a halt. They seized him, forced him into their vehicle and took him to an undisclosed secret site. There they stripped Cheema naked, tied him so tightly that he could barely breathe, and beat him for a half hour with a wooden rod and leather strap (Cheema 2010).

The physical torture was followed by humiliation tactics. Cheema's captors shaved him, including his head and eyebrows, and forced him into degrading positions while photographing him. "'This is the consequence of writing against the government,' they said, then warned him of more torture and public posting of the photos, should he utter a word of the events in the media. Cheema found himself dumped 100 kilometers outside of Islamabad, the city that he called home (ibid.).

Cheema's offense was more specific than that. He had already taken on the Pakistani Parliament, finding that 70 percent of parliamentarians had not paid their taxes. But the articles that ostensibly triggered the torture were about the intelligence agencies: "They operate without any lawful authority, and this is something people at large don't know, that our agencies didn't have any law to govern the assumptions, so I started highlighting that," he explained (ibid.).

Cheema had investigated what appeared to be corrupt processes involving the very top level generals, the army's chief security, and he criticized the justice system in its trial of terror suspects. "Why ... are they being acquitted? ... There is no proper investigation. The evidence is not presented, so there is a problem," he said (ibid.).

Naturally, the torture left Cheema with post-traumatic stress. And in Pakistan, stigma compounded the trauma, making recovery more difficult. "That was really a painful time, and I felt very lonely," he admitted. "In our culture it is not so common that you go to the psychiatrist, and it is considered a kind of stigma that you have become so horrified. And frankly I didn't have the idea even then that one should go to the psychiatrist in the event of such a tragic happening" (Cheema 2015).

Preoccupied by their own fears, Cheema's friends "started distancing themselves from me, realizing that I am under threat," he said. "Everybody was trying to read my body language [to assess] whether I am shaken or not" (ibid.).

His terrified family could not be a source of solace either. "I was unable to share my concerns with my family, because they were already in panic," he said. They attempted to persuade him to "quit the journalism and do something else. They were very concerned about my security" (ibid.).

But quitting was not an option. Journalism was a duty for Cheema, his way of contributing to his country, and the very thing that gave his life meaning. So he pressed on with his investigations, including three more articles that called for "legislation of the [intelligence] agencies and why it is important," he said, adding, "I am not doing [journalism] for my personal glorification" (ibid.).

He also knew that all of life in Pakistan came with risk, with or without journalism. "In Pakistan many people have been killed without uttering any controversial word in their life," he said. "Yet they become victims of target killings, so if I am killed, [it is] only because I am doing what I am supposed to do ... I will have to stay firm. I am doing nothing wrong" (ibid.).

The task at hand then was to find a way through the psychological trauma. "I sometimes felt very horrified ... and I fought it out lonely ... through the post-traumatic stress," he said. "I was challenging myself, 'Be brave, be brave, you know; this is a critical time, and this time has come to test your mettle, how strong you are'" (ibid.).

Focusing on the present moment, Cheema managed his fear. Or as he said, "think less about what's going to happen [and] just think about what is happening ... My experience suggests that the more you become con-cerned about certain things, the more you think about it, the more fearful you become" (ibid.).

While Cheema mustered up his own courage, his nemeses had "blocked the supply of information by scaring [my sources] into silence, because when I was kidnapped, they took away my mobile, and obviously I was already under surveillance. They were checking who am I contacting, or [with whom] I am in touch ... So they checked my phone-book, and they went after those guys. And they [my sources] had not been in touch with me since then. And one of them, one of my key sources, had only met me for five minutes after the incident only to express regret. He was blaming himself" (ibid.).

Recognizing the events as "psychological warfare," Cheema prepared himself. "One has to be ready for it," he said. "Your enemy [sic], they are as scared as you are, so you know you just have to explore their raw nerve. Where is their raw nerve? You have to touch their raw nerve if they are doing yours" (ibid.).

Cheema was one of many journalists attacked in Pakistan. His colleague Hamid Mir was another. Known for high-level reports and interviews, including one with Osama bin Laden, Mir survived an assassination attempt. In April of 2014, after a series of death threats, a group of gunmen opened fire on Mir while he rode in his car. The first gunman shot Mir in the shoulder. Men on motorcycles drove alongside Mir's vehicle, firing the next five shots, piercing Mir's leg and organs, and left Mir unconscious (Ali and Priest 2015).

A new level of fear engulfed the profession, and most media in Pakistan went quiet, afraid of addressing the attacks. But Cheema published Mir's allegations about the suspected perpetrators—agents from Pakistan's intelligence service, the ISI [Inter-Services Intelligence]—and he continued advocating for reform, for oversight laws governing the agency. "Our news organization[s] were under attack ... I was one of the few journalists who was very vocal in his case" (Cheema 2015).

Threats and defamation against Cheema and Mir escalated and expanded, reaching Cheema's family. Callers claiming to be Taliban threatened to harm Cheema's children and alleged knowing "'where your children study, and we know where you people live,'" recalled Cheema. "I started getting panicked calls from my home" (ibid.).

Cheema managed to calm his family, assuring them that the callers were not Taliban members but impersonations by agents of the ISI, whom he believes also attacked his character. "The agency, in collaboration with their friends in the media, had launched a campaign against us," said Cheema, adding that "the ISI have traditionally been very strong in Pakistan, and speaking about them or criticizing them, it's not without risk. It's a big deal, so you must be ready for the consequences" (ibid.).

Opportunities arose for Cheema and his family to escape the throes of violence for safer countries. "I had numerous opportunities to settle in UK and US, in particular in US, but I refused," he remarked. "Look how Pakistan is in a bad shape right now … If after passing through horrible times, I still want to remain there, it means I still have hope in my country, and I hope that it will change … [and I decided that] we should try to do something great for the country and especially when it is in crisis" (ibid.).

Short of fleeing, Cheema adopted strategies of strict professionalism and magnanimity, which he argued "can mitigate the threats," even if they do not "eliminate the threats … The more professional you are, the less risk you are facing" (ibid.).

Professionalism insulates journalists from allegations that they are "using the shield of journalism for [their] own [political] purposes," a common accusation and justification for attacks, particularly by security forces if journalists "are simultaneously affiliated with political parties that are considered insurgents, or the conflict actors" (ibid.).

Rather than blaming individuals for political problems, Cheema examined systemic failures and policy weaknesses, which he argued allowed him to reveal the "problems in the system allowing all this to happen … That is also a very safe way to do it … If you put things in a bigger perspective, if you are making it policy-oriented, you are [explaining] where are the loop-holes in the system that [are] allowing this to happen" (ibid.).

While presenting important facts, Cheema insisted that professionalism requires accurately presenting all points of view, even those of his detractors. "Their grievances should also be covered," and "you don't have the luxury to misquote them," particularly when "dealing with people who are … very threatening, or who have the capability to damage you, to kill you, so you have to be more flexible [with them]" (ibid.).

These approaches, he argues, generate "a kind of feel-good factor" toward journalists. "If they want one week, or even one month [to respond], give them the time. You may be sure that they don't have anything to [say], so they are just buying time. But this buying time strategy may also win them over. They will realize that he [the journalist] is not a bad guy, actually … [Although] they may cause you some harm, but they may not like to kill you" (ibid.).

As a precautionary measure, in Pakistan, media commonly omit sensitive details, such as the names of perpetrators or victims, from their reports. For example, most media withhold names of certain militant groups in the Karachi area and refer to victims of targeted killings as "unknown persons ... No media will run the name of the party, fearing a reprisal ... preempting any backlash," explained Cheema. "They don't report even [what] they get to hear. They don't show interest to know more about it, realizing that if they cannot report [the material], what is the point to hear about them?" (ibid.).

Media organizations in Pakistan also divide reporters' duties when covering conflicts, relieving any one journalist of sole responsibility. For example, one journalist contacts the Pakistani military; another may contact the Taliban, while a third may write the story. Cheema refers to the Taliban as "the deadliest actors and the most scary" (ibid.).

Of all precautions, perhaps the most important is staying out of combat-laden territories, according to Cheema. While he acknowledged the cost of avoidance, he argued that preserving life is more important: "We don't want somebody to lose his life in pursuit of the information. Their security is equally important," he said. "If I am going there and [get] killed by [the Taliban or] killed by ISI, and at the end of the day, the world will get neither, not me, nor the information" (ibid.).

Similarly, journalists are unable to properly investigate the army or the national security establishment as they may have done in the past, admits Cheema. "When they [journalists] report the security forces, they come under threat from the insurgents, and if they report the insurgents, they come under threat from the security forces, so they are somewhere between the two ... Now there is an operation going on against target killers and the mafias in Karachi, so media is reporting with full authority [on that matter], but they cannot report about the security forces. They cannot report about the Taliban either ... In the areas where there is an insurgency going on, [there is] a kind of blanket censorship" (ibid.).

Simultaneously, journalists face censorship from profit-seeking publishers who protect advertisers for commercial reasons. "They are the major advertisers, [so] if you are reporting about them, the newspaper, the media will not run any story, because they are the advertisers; they give the revenue," explained Cheema (ibid.).

Despite the confines of journalism in Pakistan, Cheema is determined to work toward a more just and peaceful Pakistan. "When your country is in crisis, when it is not in a good shape, you become more concerned about your country, and you want to do something for it," he said. "Pakistan is unfortunately a crisis country, and every day we get to know [that more]—although the situation has changed a lot in the last 20 years. Nevertheless, we are not new to the stories about the blasts, or the targeted killing in different parts ... It is not a normal situation, [although] it was a kind of new normal for Pakistanis" (ibid.).

As described in "On the Origin of Stories" (Chapter 2), Cheema continues to investigate a wide range of sensitive subjects, such as rampant tax evasion among Pakistani parliamentarians, an issue he said was "very close to my heart … I took on the whole parliament, bringing to attention, unmasking the tax evading members of parliament by showing their tax records. All the names were named, and we found out that 70 percent of them did not file their tax returns. Included among them was the president of Pakistan and half of the cabinet. This story made international headlines" (ibid.).

Similar to Pakistan, Mexico features regions mired in violence, corruption, and lawlessness. The two countries also share high rankings as some of the most dangerous countries for journalists, where attacks are rampant and gruesome. In the past decade, more than 80 journalists lost their lives in Mexico, while another 17 have disappeared, according to Reporters without Borders (2015b). Hundreds more have been attacked, according to London-based NGO, Article 19, which chronicled 303 such attacks in just the first nine months of 2015 (Article 19 2015). Journalists like the award-winning Sandra Rodriguez Nieto have sought to understand the causes and solutions to Mexico's systemic poverty, violence, and corruption.

Reporting in Mexico

Even before Mexico's Ciudad Juarez became known as the "murder capital of the world," hundreds of women and girls were being mysteriously murdered. Crime worsened in the border city, reaching 1,500 murders in 2008, 2,650 in 2009 and 3,100 in 2010. As the city increasingly resembled a war-zone, approximately 300,000 people fled (Chapparo 2015).

Not content with reporting events and incidents, investigative journalist Sandra Rodriguez Nieto sought to understand the underlying causes of the violence, corruption, and crime. "These people are suffering for something deeper than an anecdote for some crime," she said (Rodriguez Nieto 2014).

Beneath the tragic stories and superficial explanations about organized crime and gang violence, Rodriguez Nieto suspected deeper, less visible factors were causing the suffering of her fellow citizens. "It's not just a problem of people killing other people. It's [a question of] why we are reaching these levels of violence. This is just one symptom of a very complicated problem," she explained. "My idea was to connect these stories, these crime stories to bigger forces" (ibid.).

Observing the city's urban design, Rodriguez Nieto suspected that even geography played a role in the murders. "You may have a housing project here [in one spot] and then hectares empty and then another housing project," she explained. With housing so scattered, "the people have to walk through a very hostile landscape, so if you see the landscape of the city, you may understand why it's so violent ... So I started to investigate ... [using] public [property] records, maps, access officers to see who these empty lands belong to" (ibid.).

"After several tries," Rodriguez Nieto discovered "that these lands belong to former politicians who were, in the last 30 years, selling land to Maquiladoras (factories) and expanding the city with public money for services and forcing the people to live farther and farther apart every year—with very high human costs" (ibid.).

If geography was one element contributing to high murder rates, Rodriguez Nieto also suspected governance systems. To investigate the justice system, she created an "index of impunity" comparing the "crime versus investigations or sentences to understand how high the [level of] impunity was and how this impunity is working in the society, like sending the message that you can kill, and there [are] no consequences" (ibid.).

The failures of the justice system were astonishing. "97% of the killings in Ciudad Juarez remain unsolved. So who killed these people? Nobody can say. [It] could be the army ... could be the federal police ... could be anyone," she said, adding, "We have tons of cases, unsolved cases of police and prosecutors and governors involved with organized crime. That's Mexico. And I think it's [clearer] now than before with the events in Guerrero: The local government gave the order to kidnap 43 students. But that is a very common situation in Mexico" (ibid.).

While impossible to prove culpability for the killings, Rodriguez Nieto's work noted two revelations: First, the "calibers" used were of a particular type, "for the exclusive use of the army," she explained. And perhaps more importantly, "They [the government] didn't do anything to stop this [killing]. They are not even investigating this, not even [opening] the files with these crimes ... Political power has the power to stop this, and they were just not doing it ... [and] society doesn't have any way to [hold] government accountable for these kinds of things, for impunity, for corruption. So nothing is solved" (ibid.)

The troubling effect of growing impunity in Mexico is that "anybody can kill in this environment. And that's the worst scenario because it's anybody, literally anybody," explained Rodriguez Nieto (ibid.).

Through public records, she then traced the illegal weapons trade, discovering that "the government was not stopping the influx of weapons into the country, like at all. They were seizing like three guns per year or something" (ibid.).

With insight about the flow of illegal weapons, a crippled justice system and a dangerous topography, Rodriguez Nieto studied what she believed was the key factor and final puzzle piece to the problems of Ciudad Juarez—the global economic system—which had ostensibly crumbled the local economy and left people in dire poverty. "In Juarez it's clear, for instance, after Liemann Brothers collapsed in 2007 or 2009 ... A lot of factories closed in the city, like the next day. So it's very easy to observe," she said. "You can see the effects of global policies in human life" (ibid.).

Rodriguez Nieto traced the "chain of damages" in her country from the time China joined the World Trade Organization. At that time, factories that had been employing Mexicans fled for China, leaving a domino effect on the community. "You could see in the city, the people struggling for work because of some plant [that] just left for China … For instance, this factory worker is unemployed, so she stopped buying shoes. She stopped buying coffee. She stopped sending the kids to school. She stopped using this bus. The bus driver stopped," she explained, describing the "chain of effects" on the "whole city that relies on the Maquiladora model" (ibid.).

The impoverished citizens of Ciudad Juarez, once victims of the economic collapse, then became the victims of violence, she said. Through building another data set, Rodriguez Nieto deconstructed the government's claims about the "criminals" who had been killed. "The government was saying all of the victims are 'criminals' … that 'we are killing criminals' … or [that] they were killed by criminals … [But they were] just poor people, unarmed civilians … The evidence is that [these people were] just poor kids, mostly kids, or just mostly young males from the poorest neighborhoods, unarmed civilians," she said. "And if they were in the drug business, they were in the lowest, lowest part of the chains" (ibid.).

As women and girls disappeared from Ciudad Juarez, Rodriguez Nieto generated another database to analyze the patterns associated with their abductions and deaths. "I found a pattern in the cases that pointed out that they were being kidnapped in a very specific part of the city, a very specific part of the city connected with many other crimes happening at that time … related to the drug business," and they occurred "specifically in one part of the city … in Juarez downtown" (ibid.).

Though Rodriguez Nieto's stories revealed the complexities behind the descent of Ciudad Juarez, she contends that her "most important story" was "when the army was deployed into the city, which is known as the beginning of the battle for the city," she said. "It was terrible. They [were] arresting people [and] violating the constitution … As a journalist, I knew that it was my duty, my honor I could say, to cover that. It was the best [assignment]" (ibid.).

In 2008, the raging battle for the streets of Ciudad Juarez arrived at Rodriguez Nieto's news organization, *El Diario de Juárez*, killing her colleague "in my newsroom." The incident brought home the realities of Juarez and the hazards of reporting in Mexico. But rather than chilling journalism, the incident "gave me more strength and the decision to keep on reporting, trying to understand," she said. "All of us, not just to me, but to all of my colleagues at *El Diario de Juárez*, we [were] all convinced that we were not scared, that we were angry, and we wanted justice and that we were working until we could [find justice]. And I think that we all did what we could … We all knew that we could die. But you don't think about it actually, because you are there, and when you don't feel the danger, you are feeling that ... the duty is first" (ibid.).

Instead of thinking of her own possible fate, Rodriguez Nieto "focused on the importance of the story ... I didn't think of any other thing. I just thought I have to be the best that I can because there is nobody else covering the army, for instance ... [I didn't think of my] well-being until later" (ibid.).

That ethic, she argues, is widespread in her profession. "I think any journalist would have done the same in my position," she said. "I remember one day writing an article and I thought, I'm the only person ever to do this at this moment in the city. And I thought that was a huge responsibility. And I just thought that I wanted to be good enough for ... like a witness. That was my concern" (ibid.).

As a precautionary measure, the newspaper's management eliminated the journalists' bylines, which Rodriguez Nieto said created a separate set of problems. "Sometimes you have a lot of mistakes, and we were not bylining," she said, adding, "It was kind of crazy ... We were entirely unprepared, and we were reckless with many security protocols. I mean we were totally unprepared for that level of violence" (ibid.).

In Rodriguez Nieto's view, a more effective safety measure is strict adherence to objective reporting. Reporters should be "wiser with information, not to say something that you cannot prove, or not to say something that sounds personal, or not to say something out of context, like 'these people [are] bad.' No, no, this is a *system* of crime, etcetera. I think that's more important than taking physical precautions like a bullet-proof vest or something" (ibid.).

The practice also supported her "own mental health. I was trying to be very scrupulous, trying to be the most responsible [that] I could" (ibid.). As one example, when reporting about intergroup killings, rather than focusing on the "winning" group that was "killing everybody," she wrote about both gangs within a larger context. "I could have written just about them [the victorious], but for precaution, I included the other group," she said, which suggests that "I'm not taking sides. I'm identifying everybody as I can ... in order to make it clear that it was not personal because the most dangerous thing is [when] some criminal might think that you are working for money and not as a reporter" (ibid.).

Journalists in Mexico also refrained from publishing information such as "people's names, etcetera," said Rodriguez Nieto. "It was the most dangerous kind of thing" and "kind of suicidal" (ibid.).

Some subjects and regions were also off-limits, which meant leaving "a lot of parts of Mexico" unreported: "You cannot cover" them because "it is very, very dangerous," she said. That includes "dangerous topics" such as "the involvement of government with crime, which is the most difficult and dangerous thing to expose ... and some other things in Juarez" (ibid.).

Still, nothing guaranteed safety: "I was just watching over my shoulder all the time. But I have always known, and this is very sad to tell you, but it's true: There is nothing you can do if somebody wants to kill you" (ibid.).

Rodriguez Nieto has since published her investigative findings about the power dynamics of Mexico in books that bear her name. "As much as I could [obtain] information about the protection [and] involvement of the government, I published it, and it's in my book. The participation in—of one governor at least, one Chihuahua governor—[was] involved in the organized crime. And I published it. And that was with my name" (ibid.).

Trying to solve entrenched problems in Mexico was deeply disturbing for Rodriguez Nieto, to the point where she lost hope about her work catalyzing meaningful change. But she continued reporting in an effort to contribute to the historical record.

In contrast, award-winning journalist Mae Azango refuses to relent on journalism as a change-making tool. Her home country, Liberia, is mired in widespread corruption, police misconduct, and sexual violence against women and girls (Human Rights Watch 2014), subjects that Azango sought to address through journalism.

During Liberia's civil war, local journalists had no chance for survival if they tried to report. But lessons learned during the war provided the subjects and emotional fuel for Azango's journalism. Similar to Cheema and Rodriguez Nieto, she chose her subjects in the hopes that her work might lead to alleviation of suffering and mitigate abuses of power.

Liberia remains what the NGO Freedom House calls semi-free, scoring 60 out of 100 (100 being the worst) on the freedom scale. Libel, censorship, criminal defamation laws interfere with media freedom, despite constitutional protections, punishing journalists through imprisonment and forced closures of their media companies (Freedom House 2015a; Reporters without Borders 2015a). Azango herself has been forced to flee her city and her country after reporting on controversial subjects.

Against the Tide in Liberia

Mae Azango's own suffering as a refugee informed her journalism and sensitized her to others' plights. During the Liberian civil war, "I became displaced. I became a refugee in Côte d'Ivoire," she said. "I was made less than a second class citizen, and I had no rights. My rights were violated on a daily basis" (Azango 2015).

In Côte d'Ivoire, Azango recalled being "stepped on," "slapped," "spit at" and told that "'this is not my home' on a daily basis," she said. With the flood of grievances by refugees, international protective organizations were simply too overwhelmed to address them all. "[They] had too many complaints, docket upon docket," she said. "My story wouldn't have made any difference. So I had to swallow the bitter pill while I was in Côte d'Ivoire, minding my business and behaving like a refugee until I came back home" (ibid.).

On her return to Liberia, Azango observed "people were still living the kind of life I was living in Côte d'Ivoire [but] under an elected government. It made me so angry" (ibid.).

As an "ordinary citizen," though, Azango felt powerless to "do anything" until she discovered journalism. And although she initially enrolled into the state's journalism program as a means of staying "out of trouble," she soon came to believe that "the pen was mightier than the sword. I got to realize that there was strength and power in the pen, so I said, 'oh, I think I can use this pen to shape the destiny of my country'" (ibid.).

Informed by her own experiences, Azango first investigated violence against refugees and women. "I don't like to see violence. I don't like to see people's rights being violated and most especially, women. So that is why I decided to report on mainly women, prostitution, rape, maternal health, human rights stories," she said. "When you [have been] a victim, you speak better because you went through it" (ibid.).

She also focused on exposing dangerous practices of "traditionalists" in Liberia after her own near-death experience while giving birth. At the time, during the 1990 Liberian War, "all the doctors and nurses ran away because the war had come to Monrovia," leaving Azango in the care of a traditional midwife, who insisted her delivery complications arose from unconfessed sins. "She told me I had to confess a second lover, and then the God will forgive me, and then the placenta will come out. And [that] the reason why the placenta was stuck was that I did not confess, so she beat my legs" (ibid.).

To Azango's surprise, these traditional practices were rampant, endangering women's lives. "That is why our maternal mortality rate is so high, because many are the traditional women, when the women are going under complications, they tell them to confess, and those women bleed to death. It's still going on as I speak to you, Maria. That is why we are the third country, the third highest country in maternal mortality in the world … They shouldn't be dying" (ibid.).

Female genital cutting (FGC) was another such traditional practice. But "nobody could speak about it. It was a taboo subject, so I wanted it to become a public debate," she said. "People tell me, 'oh, you don't have to talk about it; don't talk loud, somebody will get angry' … And I got so angry when I saw that 40 little children as young as two years old and [they were] circumcising them. And you are telling me not to talk, oh no. That is why I chose the subject". Even the governments of Liberia had avoided the subject, argued Azango. "No government could speak about it. That's how powerful [the taboo] was" (ibid.).

Her reports turned the abusers' wrath against her. For example, when she exposed details in the practice of FGC, the traditional communities threatened Azango and her daughter. "The traditional people came after me," she said, adding that death threats are common for discussing the forbidden subject. "If you tell, they will kill you. That's the penalty—death … They wanted to get to me to be able to get the person who confessed to me" (ibid.).

It was not until the government prohibited the practice that the threats subsided. "When the government announced it, the traditional people focused on the government. They got angry with Ellen Johnson Sirleaf's government," she said (ibid.).

With her exposés, Azango was regularly making enemies, and threats were mounting. "Whenever I write a sensitive story, I get threatened, even the story I wrote about these girls they trafficked to Lebanon. People got angry because it's a syndicate. It's a big business, and there are a lot of people in high places in my government who are part of the syndicate. Obviously they will get angry with me because I am stopping their money from flowing" (ibid.).

Azango's reports on sex slavery angered the traffickers, and her reports about police abuse antagonized the police, so much so, she believes, that "They were happy when I was in trouble … I had been reporting stories on police brutality, so the police were angry with me. So they did not protect me." But she added that her reports helped "put a policeman behind bars, because he raped a girl. I [also] made sure that I exposed some dirty police officer[s] who beat a lady, whose daughter was raped" (ibid.).

But it was her criticism of government agencies that ostensibly left her most vulnerable. "Nobody protected me," she said. "My president didn't protect me, neither did my government, neither did the police" (ibid.).

Nonetheless, Azango continued confronting injustices. "They do these things to scare me, but it doesn't scare me," she said. "Those people who are doing those things and violating people have to be brought to justice … If you are doing bad, I will go into your closet and bring it out" (ibid.).

There have been times, however, when Azango and her daughter fled Monrovia, the nation's capital. On one of those occasions, they remained in hiding for "almost a month" to evade the traditional communities who threatened to force the procedure onto her and her daughter. "If they couldn't get me, they were going to get my daughter and force her to be circumcised," she said. "I had to send her out of Monrovia to a rural area … I ran into hiding because the first law of humanity is self-preservation. If I didn't preserve my life, I wouldn't be speaking to you today" (ibid.).

Another time, she fled the country altogether "because they kept threatening my daughter. My daughter is just 11," she said. "If the people come and attack my daughter … my government wouldn't do a thing about it … That's why I took my daughter from Liberia and brought her to the US" (ibid.).

Azango's style of journalism is decidedly confrontational with an aim to facilitate change. As noted in Chapter Two, "I like to bring up these areas so my government can address [them]. That's what I do," she said. "Journalism is about making an impact, okay? So if you get into journalism and just write, write, write, and nothing comes out of it, I will tell you to change your profession … If I write a story and nothing comes out of it, I'm not journalizing ... That's what journalism is about ... [You] don't wait for the soft story. You don't sit and wait for your editor to assign you" (ibid.).

In present day Liberia, Azango has little fear about exposing wrong-doings. But there were times when such journalism was impossible, she said. In 2002, for example, when Liberia was embroiled in a vicious civil war, "everybody [was] running for their lives; people were bombarded. I was fighting for my life because I was in this area that ... the rebels were targeting," she said. "People were dying every day, so I had to stay underground, underground in a house, bolt[ed] down in the basement, because if you stay on the top floor the rocket falls through the ceiling and kill everybody ... You have to go under a concrete wall on the ground ... The streets were empty and many rockets were falling" (ibid.).

Still, Azango knows the limits of her professional pursuits and stays within their confines. And she recognizes when to retreat. "There is no story worth dying for," she said. "There are places or some stories that are so, so, so—I will emphasize this—so dangerous to cover because that story is attached to high hands in the government that can take you down at any time. [A] witch hunt is still going in my country. Though they say 'freedom of speech,' but freedom of speech is not as free as it seems. Otherwise my boss, Rodney Sieh, wouldn't have gone to jail.[8] People still disappear ... They disappear, and nobody sees them [again]. Witch-hunting is still going on in my country ... If you go and tread on dangerous waters, you will be taken out" (ibid.).

Thus, while Azango pursues controversial stories to expose iniquities in hopes of change, she refuses subjects that she believes will inevitably endanger either her or her daughter. She declined one story suggested by her "boss," because "If I take on that story to make my government look bad, so bad, I will be dead in no time. I can tell you that. There are stories that I won't do, because I don't have to die," she said. "I will be as good as dead ... I didn't get into journalism to die. I got into journalism to create a debate, and when it gets too dangerous, I go into hiding" (ibid.).

Azango factored survival into her decisions when choosing her battles, knowing she would be alone to defend herself and her daughter in light of her frequent criticism of police abuse and corruption. It was one of the inherent limitations when reporting from one's own backyard. In Russia, however, Andrei Vovk Alexeevich, Main Editor of the weekly local newspaper, *The Patriots of Nizhniy*, faced a completely different set of limitations. And in contrast, he worked side-by-side with local police, who in turn worked to protect the journalists at his newspaper.

Journalism in Russia

Russia had long remained among the most dangerous countries for jour-nalists. From 1992 to 2013, some 56 journalists lost their lives in Russia, making it the fifth most dangerous country for journalists over that period of time (Committee to Protect Journalists, as reported in *Business Insider* 2014). Among the most infamous was the 2006 assassination of journalist and human rights activist Anna Politkovskaya, which shocked institutions at home and abroad. At the time, Vovk was "still quite young" and "not really formed as a journalist yet," he said. "I had some fear, mostly not even for myself for my life, but I had fear for other journalists" (Vovk 2015).

But since 2014, fewer journalists have lost their lives in Russia. "I have not heard any stories from other journalists for a long time about any threats or any killings, God forbid. So it has not been on the radar, I have not heard anything," Vovk said (ibid.).

Threats and attacks—both physical and legal—still occur, and Russia maintains a media deemed as "not free," according to the NGO Freedom House (2015b), for a variety of reasons, including political control of media content. Vovk focuses only on local issues but he, too, has "had cases for the last two–three years of threats, so some threats, they are present in my work. I still have threats," he said. "They would threaten to break my legs and arms and hands, especially they were talking about hands because I am a journalist. I need to write" (ibid.).

Although he never suffered bodily harm, "People were damaging ... either my condo or my car. People would break windows in my condo. They would damage the locks. They would damage my car. They would throw rotten fish into my condo, as in the movie Godfather. Yeah, it was an attempt to make me leave" (ibid.).

In the short-term, they succeeded, pushing Vovk out of town for months. "Since then nobody has actually claimed responsibility for those actions, so I still don't know exactly who it was, but I had to leave for half a year" (ibid.).

Both the threats and the property damage arose from stories Vovk wrote about businesses, not the government. In one story, he reported on a construction company's "schemes" to manipulate and monopolize the market, to keep prices high and competition low. "They were pretty much criminals, so they still use those [types of] methods, and they don't like when their business is covered in newspapers, in the media, because they want everything to be quiet. So when the media write about them, they don't know how to deal with it. The only way they know is to threaten and other criminal ways because they just don't know how to deal with publicity like that. They want the publicity to stop" (ibid.).

In the end, the situation "resolved" through talks. "I was quite brave, maybe even too brave," he admitted (ibid.).

Vovk and his fellow journalists frequently consult lawyers and police before publishing sensitive or inflammatory stories, such as exposing what they believe is a criminal enterprise. The story then includes police notification, which Vovk believes provides a layer of protection. "Those who read the story, they actually can see that it is not only me as a single journalist who knows all this, but it is actually already even the police and other people who are involved, so I am safer" (ibid.).

Maintaining close, symbiotic ties to law enforcement is a common practice among journalists at Vovk's publication. "Our police learned to cooperate with journalists. And because journalists actually help police, and it's kind of a symbiotic, protective relationship," he explained. "For example, if the police is looking for some suspects and provides a photo or some kind of drawing or sketch of a suspect, journalists spread this information through the newspapers, or police can spread information through journalists about people who have disappeared ... And sometimes relatives actually can find people because of that, because journalists usually help by publishing that information. It's more [that] information comes from the police and gets published" (ibid.).

Neither Vovk nor his close colleagues cover national or international politics, instead focusing on local, municipal issues. "We do not criticize the national government, and I almost never see any criticism of the national government in regional newspapers or media," primarily because "nobody really believes that it makes sense or it will change anything to criticize the national government," he explained. "At the national level we have stricter policies, and they are based on vertical power, so we don't really have the same mechanism for change [as with local politics]. We had some examples where we could still influence federal decisions ... But they happen more rarely" (ibid.).

Another complication is the confusing nature of national politics, he added. "We don't really understand a lot of decisions at the federal level, and this lack of understanding is the main reason [we avoid covering it]. So it's a kind of gap or disconnect between [our] regions and the Moscow-level, the national-level, and not everything is understandable and accessible for us" (ibid.).

Vovk and his colleagues instead focus on issues that they think their reporting can affect. "We try to change life but at the regional level, not national," he said. For example, journalists at Vovk's newspaper challenged the local government's decisions to cut benefits for poor people and close libraries. In the former, "after we started to investigate it and to write about it, the government retracted and decided not to go ahead with that decision, so that decision was cancelled, so now the subsidies stay in place" (ibid.).

While fear for their lives may not hinder journalists' freedoms as it may have in years prior, career concerns constrain them, according to Vovk. Many media are owned by either oligarchs or politicians, who interfere with editorial decisions. "Currently a lot of newspapers are actually owned by politicians, and different political holdings divide the newspapers and have their influence among them. So we don't really have that many purely commercial newspapers trying to make money anymore. But mostly newspapers are now owned and controlled by some political figures who are promoting their own agendas," he explained. "It's not even political parties per se, because we are moving away from the political party system, based on party influence. But we have big influential businessmen, entrepreneurs and businessmen, and they want to promote their commercial interests. And in order to be successful in business, they need to be politicians. And then to be a successful politician, they have to have their own media to promote their agenda, so it's kind of this blended businessman, politician, owner of media" (ibid.).

Ownership structure creates multiple problems, including blanket prohibitions on particular subjects, mostly those related to the owners. "They will tell us, 'okay, you understand that [the newspaper] is owned by such and such people, so you won't be able to write bad things about those people' ... so some topics are [just] not going to happen" (ibid.).

At his own publication, Vovk finds himself constantly haggling with owners over stories and censorship. "As an editor I pretty much struggle with the owners every week when I plan a new issue, what topics to include. So it happens a lot" (ibid.).

Vovk still manages to persuade the owners. "As an editor I know which topics not to suggest," he said. But sometimes I persuade them that the topic is really important and might change something [and be] beneficial to them as well. Sometimes [it] even happens that the topic is actually accepted" (ibid.).

After they plan the publication, however, the stories can still be censored. "Somebody just censors what we write," he said (ibid.).

Journalists concerned for their livelihoods self-censor in self-preservation. "A person coming to [work for] that media [organization] already knows that there is some limit. And also another self-censorship when it's not prohibited per se, but the journalist might think, 'okay if I write some negative things about something or somebody, I might be either fired or somehow punished.' And it is a crisis, economic crisis, [because] the jobs are scarce. Some media are being closed, so people have to sometimes self-censor" [ibid].

These are the hallmarks of the local danger zone journalists interviewed for this research. Although foreign correspondents share similar emotions and commitments, for local journalists, they are more personal: It is their home and their friends and family who suffer. While foreign correspondents slip in and out of danger zones, local journalists remain under sustained challenges, searching for ways to make a "better society," according to interviews. Their situations vary in the particulars, but the desire to better their societies remains constant.

Notes

1 The Provisional IRA emerged after the Official IRA disbanded.
2 The unnamed journalists in this chapter, such as IJ1–IJ7, are journalists who have not consented to have their identities revealed.

3 The UVF or Ulster Volunteer Force, was a loyalist "paramilitary" organization.
4 The UDA or the Ulster Defence Association was a loyalist paramilitary or vigilante organization.
5 Gerry Adams is an elected parliamentarian and president of Sinn Fein, the party that represented the IRA.
6 Martin McGuinness is an elected parliamentarian who was an acknowledged leader in the Provisional IRA.
7 http://tribune.com.pk/story/815075/pakistan-most-dangerous-country-for-journa lists-in-2014-report/.
8 Sieh was jailed for a story claimed to be libelous.

References

Ali, Idrees and Dana Priest. 2015. "Living Like a Fugitive: Pakistan's most famous TV journalist, Hamid Mir, is undeterred from reporting despite ongoing threats and an ambush by gunmen." *The Washington Post*. July 25. http://www. washingtonpost.com/sf/investigative/2015/07/25/living-like-a-fugitive/. Accessed March 20, 2016.

Article 19. 2015. December 18. https://www.article19.org/resources.php/resource/ 38228/en/dario-ramirez-to-step-down-as-article-19-director-for-mexico-and-central-america. Accessed March 20, 2016.

Azango, Mae. 2015. Personal Interview. Via Telephone from Auckland to Pennsylvania. September 2.

Chapparo, Luis. 2015. "If Ciudad Juarez is 'Back,' Why Haven't the Killings Stopped?" https://news.vice.com/article/if-ciudad-juarez-is-back-why-havent-the-killings-stopped. Accessed March 20, 2016.

Cheema, Umar. 2010. "Abducted and Tortured—for Reporting the News: 'This is the consequence of writing against the government,' my captors said." *Wall Street Journal*. October 13. http://www.wsj.com/articles/SB100014240527487037 94104575545914180906100. Accessed March 20, 2016.

Cheema, Umar. 2015. Personal Interview. Via Skype. Auckland to Islamabad. August 17.

Committee to Protect Journalists. 2014. As cited in "These Charts Show how Journalism Has Turned into a Hazardous and even Deadly Profession throughout the World." *Business Insider*, August 21. http://www.businessinsider.com/these-are-the-most-dangerous-countries-for-journalists-2014-8. Accessed March 20, 2016.

Freedom House. 2015a. "Liberia." https://freedomhouse.org/report/freedom-press/ 2015/liberia. Accessed March 20, 2016.

Freedom House. 2015b. "Russia." https://freedomhouse.org/report/freedom-press/ 2015/russia. Accessed March 20, 2016.

Human Rights Watch. 2014. "World Report 2014: Liberia." https://www.hrw.org/ world-report/2014/country-chapters/liberia. Accessed March 20, 2016.

IJ1. 2009. Personal Interview. In Person. Belfast. August.

IJ2. 2009. Personal Interview. In Person. Belfast. August

IJ7. 2010. Personal Interview. In Person. Belfast. August.

Kurspahic, Kemal. 2014. Personal Interview. In Person. Tyson's Corner, VA. November 3.

McCann, Eamonn. 2009. Personal Interview. In Person. Belfast. August.

McGinley, Martin. 2009. Personal Interview. In Person. Derry, Northern Ireland. August.

McGinley, Martin. 2010. Personal Interview. In Person. Derry, Northern Ireland. September.

McKittrick, David. 2009. Personal Interview. In Person. Belfast. August.

McLaughlin, Terry. 2009. Personal Interview. In Person. Belfast. August.

Mallie, Eamonn. 2009. Personal Interview. In Person. Belfast. August.

Mallie, Eamonn. 2010. Personal Interview. In Person. Belfast. August.

Pakistani Press Foundation. 2015. "No Country for Journalists." November 26. http://www.pakistanpressfoundation.org/2015/11/no-country-for-journalists/. Accessed December 31, 2015.

Reporters without Borders. 2015a. http://en.rsf.org/liberia.html. Accessed December 31, 2015.

Reporters without Borders. 2015b. http://en.rsf.org/report-mexico.184.html. Accessed December 31, 2015.

Rodriguez Nieto, Sandra. 2014. Personal Interview. Via Skype. Los Angeles to Mexico City. November 17.

Vovk, Andrei. 2015. Personal Interview. Via Skype. Auckland to Nizhniy, Russia. November.

6   The First Casualty

> Whenever anybody locks the doors on [media] coverage, you know that
> something terrible is going on inside.
>   Roy Gutman on discovering the concentration camps in Bosnia

It's a shift from the years when combatants sought the sympathies of
traditional journalists to tell their stories, express their grievances and
communicate with foes, friends, and potential supporters. With the
internet at their fingertips, combatants now bypass traditional legacy
media to distribute their unfiltered messages—inclusive of cute cat
photos, selfies, and public displays of gruesome murders, which are
designed to attract, persuade, or project power.

No longer necessary in this role, traditional journalists have become dis-
posable, problematic, or a tool to extort money and project power for some
groups, such as the Islamic State, which seek to control their own narratives.
In the new scheme, neutral journalists are, as veteran correspondent
Carol Williams said, "at best ... in the way" (The Scholars' Circle 2012).
They are useful when managed, disseminating "our" stories, abiding by
"our" rules, and a nuisance when they do not. Information controllers
constrain journalists through access restrictions, censorship, spin, and
the chilling effects of punishment, whether by expulsions, violence,
incarceration or death.

This chapter explores how foreign correspondents navigate through a
maze of restrictions in efforts to wrest some piece of truth or truths from
the clutches of their suppressors. They negotiate for access, and rely on
resourcefulness, stealth, and a healthy dose of determination in their
struggles to find and tell their stories. "We've got to find ways around all
of these blockades that we've got," declared Roy Gutman. "There are
ways around it. But we have to find those ways. You have to define the
problem. And the problem is that the doors are closed ... [But] journalists
have to do this" (Gutman 2014).

Historically, as now, "Access comes with rules, [and] the people that make
the rules are the guys who have the guns," explained Pulitzer Prize-winning

journalist and journalism professor Michael Parks. "That hasn't changed" (Parks 2014).

Much has changed, however, including the "guys who have the guns," the prosecution of war, the terrain, and the technology.

Changing Rules of Access

As noted in "Staying Alive," (Chapter 4) before the age of terror, journalists like Terry McCarthy had "carte blanche" to travel by bus or car between the military and rebel territories to interview adversaries and witness first-hand the events during conflict. "I remember we used to have t-shirts which said [in Spanish], 'Don't shoot me, I'm a journalist.' And it was kind of a joke because there was no question in those days that anyone would shoot a journalist because we were independent," said McCarthy. "You were a non-combatant, and both sides respected that. You could literally cross the lines" (The Scholars' Circle 2012; McCarthy 2014).

In the wars of Central America, for example, McCarthy drove "into the highlands" of El Salvador to "meet the guerrillas and talk to them. And then you'd drive back in the afternoon and meet the army on the government side, and there was no threat to you. That wasn't sanctionable; the government didn't go after journalists who tried to do that" (McCarthy 2014).

In the Chechen War, rebels organized meetings with journalists who were their conduits to the rest of the world. "The Chechen militants would usually arrange to meet with the journalists from outside of Russia in some surreptitious way," recalled Carol Williams. In one incident, she recalled, "[They] took over this village, and it was completely surrounded by 10,000 Russian troops, a little village of like, 88 people, and maybe an equivalent number of Chechens or probably less, more like 50. And ... [they] sent a bus out to collect us all and take us into the town, to meet the leader" (Williams 2014).

Historically, in more conventional conflicts, foreign correspondents usually covered one side and sometimes held a rank of officer in the military, according to Parks. "We were accredited correspondents, had little cards. I still have one somewhere that said I was an American, a civilian serving with US forces, and I had the assimilated rank of major. And then they promoted all of us bureau chiefs to colonels. The importance of that was getting on aircraft. People got on aircraft according to their assignments and according to ranks. So it was important to travel around because we were traveling on military aircraft for the most part," he explained. "In fact, if you look at World War II and the Korean War— [in] World War II, the correspondents were in uniform, and they were again majors, and on their little gold leaf insignia for a major was a 'C,' [for] 'correspondent.' Covering from the German side? No. Were they having discussions with German officials? No. Were they able to accompany Soviet troops, the Red Army as it rolled into Germany? No. Soviet correspondents did [that]" (Parks 2014).

That was a time of "set-piece war journalism," according to David Schlesinger. Clarity about adversaries' identities, territories, and frontlines simplified reporting duties. "When you had wars with two clearly defined sides, with clearly defined frontlines, and journalists who, whatever their objectivity, or commitment to objectivity might be, clearly came from one side or the other and tended to report from that side" (Schlesinger 2014).

Limitations still persisted. For example, during the Vietnam War, "you couldn't go to the Viet Cong and talk to them. [But] you could go to Paris and talk to the peace talk delegation. I did go to Hanoi, which took some time to organize. But no, you couldn't talk to all sides easily. One could go to the North Vietnamese embassy in Thailand and have a pleasant cup of tea," explained Parks. "Again, it's guys with guns who make the rules. If they see it to their advantage, if you can persuade them that they have a story to be told, often they'll let you in" (Parks 2014).

During the Cold War, foreign correspondents covering the Soviet Union were confined to Moscow. "The Soviet military had it entirely sealed off," said Williams. "You also had to have permission to travel outside of Moscow, and they would just reject it, sometimes for the obvious reasons, but sometimes for just ridiculous reasons why you couldn't go ... And back then, the government controlled every means of transport, and the Soviet Union was such a vast territory you couldn't even infiltrate. They didn't have rental cars and stuff like that" (Williams 2014).

A vehicle didn't guarantee transportation either, as Williams learned on a planned road trip. She and a *Washington Post* colleague faced daunting obstacles despite securing a car for a trek to the Black Sea. "I could've written a novel from our experiences on this five day trip. There were fuel shortages everywhere. You couldn't buy gas anywhere. And we'd forgotten that when you go anywhere outside of Moscow, spare parts for Russian-made cars are in deficit, so it was considered okay to steal your windshield wipers and your gas-caps and your rear view mirror. We had to, by hook or by crook, bribe people to give us windshield wipers when ours got stolen" (ibid.).

Soviet officials also closely monitored and escorted journalists covering Afghanistan during the 1980s, which Williams covered three times. "The Soviet Foreign Ministry would decide periodically, 'oh well, we want to show them how well we have everything under control there,'" she said. "You were taken around by busloads. You know, it was not a one-on-one situation. They always had translators, so you could talk to the Afghans in the market ... Soviet-supplied Afghans who were loyal to the occupation" (ibid.).

Clarity about the combatants and territories made journalists' jobs less complicated, according to Vice News' Andrew Glazer. "When Dan Rather covered the Vietnam War, or when war reporters used to cover the first invasion of Iraq, there were clear delineations ... It was either one state versus another state, or it was one group versus another group ... Now everything is so fragmented, and we're not talking about states anymore. You don't necessarily know who the parties are, and it's not—you can't go from front to [another] front with the cooperation of both sides who want to tell their story. [There] used to be neutral territory. It's no longer states that are fighting each other. We're in a post-state world" (Glazer 2014).

In many cases, journalists simply asked for access from officials, military or rebel leaders. "You went out and you presented yourself to the senior officer, who said, 'Okay. You can hang around,'" said Parks. "[Journalists] can go and find someone who would let them in (Parks 2014).

But in the wireless information age, officials can instantly size-up journalists with a quick internet search, as discovered by historian and *Al Jazeera* columnist Mark LeVine on a return trip to Bahrain. In 2010 after a Saudi invasion, LeVine had easily entered the country despite security concerns. "I showed up in Bahrain without a visa, and they looked at me a little funny, [but] they still let me in. And that was when the Saudis invaded" (The Scholars' Circle 2012).

His 2011 return, however, was not quite so smooth. "I spoke to the Bahraini embassy before I left [the US], and they said, 'no, no, you don't need a visa. Just show up.'" But when LeVine arrived, at roughly 3 am, the Bahraini border control agents "went on their smart phone, and that was the end of that. I didn't get out of the airport" (ibid.).

Similar data gave LeVine pause before returning to other Middle East countries, for fear of putting "a lot of people in danger," he said, adding, "every single government in the region has reason to and can very easily find out who you are ... They can Google me in one second. So if they don't want to let you in—and if they do let you in because you have extensive contacts, then you're being monitored. So your freedom to move and meet with people is constricted. It's much harder now to do the work journalists desperately need to be doing" (ibid.).

Mounting Dangers

The wars in the former Yugoslavia may have been a harbinger of what was to come. Snipers and other fighters turned their guns onto journalists. But still, journalists "could go over to the Serb side almost all the time, even when NATO was threatening to bomb, and you could get around," said Allan Little. "You would be restricted and humiliated, intimidated and so on ... [but] the main danger was being caught in crossfire, being in the wrong place at the wrong time. And enough of my friends were killed for that to be no small thing at the time. But you could go there without being worried that you'd end up with your throat cut. You can't do that now" (Little 2015).

Instead of engaging journalists to tell their stories, exhibition killings have become a means for extremist groups to "advertise their prowess, their jihadist prowess," according to Little. "They're saying to jihadi groups around the world, 'we're the ones, we're the champions; send us your money. Send us your young men. Send us your weapons. We're at the forefront. We're the cutting edge of the fight for global jihad.' So there's a market among them for attention and profile and renown and prowess. So the lives of journalists have become valuable commodities in the pursuit of this, in the pursuit of primacy in the global jihad" (ibid.).

In Little's experience, entire swaths of Afghanistan, under control of jihadists, are now simply too dangerous to cover. "For years and years, the only territory in Afghanistan that was accessible was the territory that's controlled securely by Western-backed governments. So you could fly to Herat from Kabul, [but] you can't drive there," he said. It's a "situation of lawlessness … and has been now for years" (ibid.).

Penetrating Afghanistan beyond the major cities would be "suicidal," he added. "So we can't get cover anymore. The only thing you can do there is talk to people who have recently come from those areas into government-controlled areas and ask them what the situation is like. You can't go yourself. So when, for example, a NATO bomb lands and wipes out an extended family, once upon a time it was possible to [go into] the village to seek eye-witness reports to verify what had happened. And you can't do that anymore" (ibid.).

McCarthy concurred. "After 9/11 all bets were off … You can't just get a bus in from Jordan or Pakistan and set up in a youth hostel. You'd get killed, or you'd get kidnapped" (McCarthy 2014).

This inability for journalists to physically witness and report is "hurting journalism" because of the "inability of open-minded, balanced reporters to get into these places and see for themselves and report in an unbiased manner" (Williams 2014).

Still, however, journalists such as McCarthy argue "Journalism is all about finding a way" (McCarthy 2014).

Finding a Way

Armed guards block roads and screen checkpoints throughout danger zones, barring access. Some find their ways nonetheless, leaning on resourcefulness, charm offensives or stealth, sometimes aided by persuasion, gifts, false identification, or winning story ideas.

After 9/11, New Zealand-based freelance journalist, Jon Stephenson began his journey into Afghanistan with a flight to India, a train to the

Pakistani border, and a long walk into Pakistan. "I just walked across the border. Wagah, the border between Pakistan and India, is quite a long walk," he said. "From the moment I arrived in Pakistan, I started collecting info on what the locals felt ... on buses, and even in a hotel, I'd talk to the hotel clerk and ... I met an MP from the Pakistani parliament. He invited me to his home in Islamabad. I interviewed the Saudi ambassador to Pakistan who I met on the roof of the Marriott being interviewed by CNN. And I just sort of started there really and worked my way up" (Stephenson 2014).

Arriving in Peshawar, close to the Afghanistan border, Stephenson "just asked around and tried to find out who was going in [to Afghanistan]." There he met "the family of Abdul Haq, who was one of the major resistance leaders during the so called jihad against the Soviets ... I ended up in his family's compound in Peshawar, and there were a couple of other journalists there as well, one guy I think from Germany, another guy from Paris" (ibid.).

The Haq family guided the journalists into Afghanistan. "We were based in Jalalabad in the Eastern part of Afghanistan. It was very close to the Khyber Pass. And I spent most of my time at a place called Tora Bora which was the last major battle of the war and the place where bin Laden was before he escaped across the mountains to Pakistan," Stephenson recalled. "We went up with some of the locals. I think [the American journalist] bribed them, but I just tagged along. We walked into the mountains until we got to the stage where we were a significant distance from the other journalists, maybe two kilometers away from them and about 800 meters from Al Qaeda. We got mortared that first day" (ibid.).

During the Iraq War, Stephenson tried a different tack, entering as a "humanitarian," not as a journalist. "I went from Amman to Baghdad during the war, and I basically fooled the Iraqis at the embassy in Amman and said I was a humanitarian. I sort of fudged it. I don't know what they thought I was in the end, although I'm sure they worked out that I was a journalist. But I got to Baghdad, and it was the last ten days of the war, and I pretty much stayed under the radar until things were out of control. And no one really cared about one [journalist]" (ibid.).

The strategy worked for Stephenson who managed to report from the war-torn country while other journalists were locked out. For example, correspondents from the Australian Broadcasting Corporation (ABC) whom "I'd met previously in Afghanistan ... they couldn't get in," he said (ibid.).

Entering Iraq has been problematic at other points in history, even before modern Gulf Wars, according to Parks, who was "denied visas for years," he said. But in 1977, Parks entered by tagging along with the United Nations' Secretary General, Kurt Waldheim. "I was on his plane. So [I] got in that way" (Parks 2014).

In 2012, Danny Gold entered Northern Iraq with the help of a colleague. "I had a really good friend [who] was Kurdish, and he had been a 'fixer' at *The New York Times*. He was very well connected there [in Northern Iraq]," he explained. "We worked together, and I knew a bit about Kurdish history, and Kurds love anyone who knows anything about them ... We both had a feeling that things were changing for the Kurds. They were getting more powerful, and it turned out to be really true. They're sort of the darling of the media right now. But this is like late 2012, and no one cared about them ... I had his contacts, so I went over there on my own in August 2012" (Gold 2014).

Because of the contacts, getting into "Northern Iraq was pretty easy. It's a good starting point because Kurds welcome Westerners. They welcome journalists," explained Gold. "The Kurds [there], they're all welcoming for the most part". But after reporting from Northern Iraq, Gold wanted to cover the conflict in Syria, which turned out to be much more difficult to access (ibid.).

Finding a Way into Syria

Gold had been denied entry into Syria "the first few times." So after a good experience with the Iraqi Kurds, he and an Italian photographer approached a Kurdish group in Syria, in hopes of a similar welcome. "There were differences between the Kurdish parties in power in Iraq and the Kurdish party in power in Syria. There's a rivalry," he said. "We kept getting told we needed special permissions, and we couldn't get them from anyone. No one was giving [permission]. So we went back and forth, barging through officials' doors, and we couldn't get anything ... We were desperate. We were losing our minds, and we were in this hotel in some crappy town in Kurdistan" (ibid.).

There at the hotel, Gold and his colleague met staff from nonprofit organization, Human Rights Watch, who had just returned from Syria, fueling Gold's decision to try again, to "see what happens. So we went to the border, and we kept getting checked," said Gold. "It took a lot of time for us to get permission; it was pretty crazy ... [Eventually], the people there [at the border] were like, 'you know what, we don't care,' and they just let us through" (ibid.).

With one last checkpoint to cross into Syria, which was "just like some sand dune in the desert," the Iraqi military stopped the journalists. "We were getting through, and the Iraqi forces stopped us. They're like, 'what are you doing?' ... It was tense because we'd driven over there, and we didn't know where we were. We didn't know whether we were in Kurdish Iraq territory or Iraqi Iraq territory, which is a bad look if you're two journalists, two Western journalists ... It was nerve-racking" (ibid.).

Surprisingly, the Iraqi military simply invited the journalists to join them. "They were like, 'You know what, come with us' ... just come with us for a night and stay with us for a night'" recalled Gold. "They ended up taking us [across] at night," allowing them through the checkpoint but warned, "Just make sure your guys are on the other side" (ibid.).

Once in Syria, the journalists encountered another group of Kurds, whom they could not identify as "either refugees or smugglers, smuggling cigarettes or gas," said Gold. "They ran from us at first because they thought we were [part of the military] forces. Then they came back ... And a truck came with a gun on the back, and that became our guide with the forces to protect us. And we just started from there" (ibid.).

It wasn't the last time Gold would enter Syria. Another time, the "border kept getting shut down because of the fighting," he said. Without a group to help them cross, the journalists paid smugglers to take them across. "Their idea of smuggling was dropping us off in a field and saying like, 'okay, go, run!' so we ran across the field, but that wasn't the hard part. The hard part was coming back into Turkey, because the Turks are assholes about that. Our guide was like, 'everything is no problem, no problem, no problem.' Every fixer ... 'no problem, we got this.' But it's always a problem" (ibid.).

Sneaking in had a consequence: Gold and his colleagues found themselves in a Turkish detention facility. "We thought we had gotten banned from Turkey ... We got caught, sat in a guy's office," he recalled. But the official "knew Italian, so he and my colleague started talking" and eventually the agent relented. "[He] was like, 'alright, we didn't see you, and you didn't see us.' And that all worked out pretty well" (ibid.).

Other journalists have snuck into Syria more stealthily. One Syrian American journalist reportedly got into the Northern part of the country with her video camera by hiding inside a barrel that was pulled across the river. She "encountered what is now called ISIS," Michael Parks, who advised her, recounted. "She took a camera in, filmed [and] was in there [for] about four days. She snuck in, snuck out. She crossed back, crossed over the river in a barrel, kind of a line pulled across, fairly harrowing" (Parks 2014).

Another journalist entered Syria via normal checkpoints from the border with Lebanon, using a borrowed Syrian identification card and her cultural knowledge, which helped her integrate and remain unnoticed among the Syrians.

False Identification and Blending In

When other avenues failed to grant access, two interviewed journalists successfully crossed borders with borrowed or fake identification. Both knew of other colleagues who had used similar strategies. "People do, people buy fake visas," said one journalist. But others denied that they or their organizations ever "misrepresented" to enter a region. "I'm a nice, middle-class boy. I don't do fake IDs," remarked Szlanko (2014).

While in Montenegro during the Yugoslav Wars, one interviewee applied for an official visa into Bosnia but was declined. "Milosevic was not letting anybody in" at the time, he recalled. "We had to buy a fake visa just to get into the country ... to get in from Montenegro" (Interview but identity withheld 2014).

PC10 borrowed a Syrian identification card to cross into Syria from Lebanon. The photo looked enough like her that she moved through each checkpoint relatively seamlessly. "Nobody ever stopped me," she said, in part because of her gender, Syrian heritage and adherence to local customs. "[Women] can fly below the radar much easier than men. For one thing, I'm covered anyway, but for women, you can always cover up ... People notice us less. We're not seen as threats" (PC10 2014).

Following local customs of each region, PC10 adhered to subtle nuances of attire to prevent conspicuousness. For example, "a couple of years ago I had to sneak into a village in Syria, which was controlled by the government and had all these checkpoints, so the first thing I had to do was take off my sunglasses because there is no way [I would pass as a local with them]," she explained. "If you go to most villages in the Middle East, people don't wear sunglasses ... In Damascus, that's a very cosmopolitan city, so my sunglasses are fine ... It's only like when you are really trying to sneak into a small village" (ibid.).

In addition to accessories and attire, PC10 matched other cultural norms as closely as possible. "I talk very much like them. I have a lot of the same habits, and I'm still a Westerner," she explained, offering an example: "When you are trying to blend in, as a woman, you kind of lean into yourself in a way that we [in the West] don't really do" (ibid.).

While PC10 snuck in to cover rebel-held areas, her colleague at the same media organization entered officially to report on government-controlled regions, with the hope that their combined reports would provide audiences a more complete picture. "He gets the visas, and he gets to go in [officially], and it's worked out great," she said, adding, "Once you sneak in and your name goes on a story, you are far less likely to get a visa" (ibid.).

Other news organizations bifurcate reporters' duties in a similar manner, partly because "If you are reporting from any of those [rebel-held] areas, it's going to be clear that you snuck in across some kind of line they don't want you to, so a lot of media has done that just to separate ... that's how people are working now ... I never wanted to cross that line, and then we always had [my colleague] who has done some coverage in opposition areas. But for the most part, he's covered government, and I've covered rebel areas" (ibid.).

While PC10 rarely uses official visas or accreditation based upon her profession, neither does she actively conceal it. "Most times I'm operating pretty openly, like not announcing that I'm a journalist, but not actually hiding it" (ibid.).

Gender worked to PC10's advantage during the Egyptian revolution as well. When her plane landed, Cairo was "under lockdown," and curfew had passed. Multiple "vigilante checkpoints" served as obstacles between the airport and her hotel. But PC10 "had met a tourist—a white guy from Canada—who flew in to see [the developments]. We decided it would be safer to go together—me, the taxi driver and him," she said. "I told the white guy to sit up front because in the Middle East, the woman is never going to sit up front" (ibid.).

At each checkpoint, "I would look down when they would come, and sometimes they wouldn't even ask for my passport. They would assume I was his wife. And he spoke for us" (ibid.).

The strategy worked for a while, but "at one point, we were stopped, and [some] people threw open the doors. And I think we were about to be taken; and one of [the vigilantes] jumped into the car, told us to drive, and got us through," (ibid.).

After a two-hour taxi ride, the driver refused to continue any further "because the hotel I was staying at was, I think, a mile or so from Tahrir Square," she said. "He's like, 'Oh I'm going to drop you off on the other side of the bridge, and it's a very quick walk' … And so he dropped us off—I don't even know where—in the middle of this bridge. And we didn't realize [that] we actually had a long, long way to go … You could not imagine what Cairo after curfew looks like … It's almost scarier sometimes than Syria because, like a war-zone, you don't know where the risks are. It goes from very, very normal to suddenly dead quiet" (ibid.).

The journalist and the tourist began the long walk over the bridge, but were stopped again, this time by a group of men on motorcycles, who demanded to search their bags. "[They said], 'We're here for your protection.' And you're completely outnumbered, so you really can't say anything. So in the middle of the bridge, they searched all our stuff," she recalled. "They drove off, and a few minutes later, they actually sent a taxi to take us to my hotel" (ibid.).

Unfortunately, the hotel was in the process of evacuating its guests. "They put us in another taxi and drove us across the Nile to the Marriott. And it was so weird … you walk in [to the Marriott], and it's like nothing is going on, like everything is normal. They're telling me about their breakfast service and their room service and this and that. And outside it feels like a war is going on, like the barbed wire and the empty streets … It's so surreal" (ibid.).

PC10 remained in Egypt for "about three weeks until after Mubarak resigned, and then I went to Libya," which in contrast to Egypt and Syria, was "super-easy. The border was open, and we just drove across with a convoy of medical workers and journalists. That was the first wave of journalists that were going in and really didn't know what the situation was, and there was a medical convoy with expat Libyans who were going in. And so a bunch of us journalists just rode on that convoy" (ibid.).

The Official Route

Gutman is among the journalists who sticks to the "official" path in attaining access: "On the whole, I try to use visas and do it legally," which means procuring passes from "whoever is in control of the area," he said. "I go to that extreme … so that means at the border, the state that you're leaving, and the state that you're entering, or the people who are in control of the other side. If you're going into a contested area, you try to get the pass from the most powerful force there, and then pray" (Gutman 2014).

A stack of press accreditations carried at all times serves as evidence of Gutman's professional standing: "among the cards I carry, I have one from the Vatican from having covered something two years ago. I have my congressional pass for pro-American areas. I have my Turkish pass. I have a pass from the separatists in Ukraine, who also give out passes. And a few others. And often my calling card is enough. But I carry those because I want to prove beyond a shadow of a doubt that I'm a journalist. And you couldn't get all those passes if [you were not a journalist], and you see that's where the risk comes in. If you don't have the passes, people [might] assume you to be working for some other agency" (ibid.).

Territory disputes mean that in many cases self-declared officials issue the visas. Carol Williams covered the Ukraine conflict: "You go to the Donetsk regional headquarters and talk to the guy who's claiming to be the new governor of the region. You have to. They don't have these functional approaches set up … They're in a defensive position, and they regard everybody who's trying to get in as an attacker, even if it's a woman in corduroys" (Williams 2014).

Williams "managed to talk [her] way into these fortresses that the rebels have created, particular regional government headquarters, and then they sandbag it and put concertina wire around it, and you have to talk your way through about three [more layers] … It's a ten-storey building [and] filthy in there, because they literally took over this building in late March or early April, and the government cut off water and electricity, so you have to walk up ten storeys of garbage-strewn stairs. And then you're up there, and they've got generators and stuff pulled in to work, and they want to give you an accreditation. You can't talk to anybody until they screen you. So you're in there for hours just to have a ten-minute conversation with somebody" (ibid.).

In Iraq, each section required a different pass, which for Dahr Jamail meant retaining a different local guide to organize them. "I had several different fixers, so if I needed to go to Sadr city I would go with this one guy who had contacts there. [For] Fallujah I would go with a woman who, her family's from there" (Jamail 2014).

Gifts and "Fees"

The custom of gifts and "fees"—such as cash, alcohol, cigarettes, or pornography—in exchange for official passes prevails in some regions, according to interviewees. One journalist said she routinely packed a little of each into her luggage, expecting officials to search her bags, remove their desired items and send her on her way. On one occasion, a border official appropriated her hot hair curlers, saying, "'oh, my wife will like these'" (C11 2014).

Alcohol and cigarettes reign. "People like [us] to get them amazing bottles of whiskey, and you know, certainly bribe people to get through," said one journalist (Interviews 2014, identity withheld). From another: "Yeah, you have to. Bring a bottle of whiskey for a government official for admission. It's like the standard in some places you go. It's understood that you're going to have to" (Interviews 2014, identity withheld).

Smaller gestures, such as offering cigarettes, candy, or bottles of water are more frequent and help build trust. "I always make sure I bring a ton of cigarettes [and] booze every now and then," said Gold. "It's just good to have. I've never gotten that recommendation from like an editor, but it's just what you do. Cigarettes make you a lot of friends" (Gold 2014).

In Africa, Gold and his colleague "gave out packs to the rebel leaders," he said. "It always helps. I mean it's a tried and true thing. It's been going on since whenever we were going overseas. Yeah, cigarettes are huge, huge. Everyone does that. It's easier. It's not even a real bribe; it's cigarettes, I mean, who cares?" (ibid.).

In Bosnia, Gutman's photographer bantered with guards while plying them with cigarettes and candy before snapping key photos, evidence of prisoner abuse. "He put them at ease by giving them cigarettes, candy, chatting with them, [and] pretending he was completely bored" (Gutman 2014).

In Syria, a rebel group asked Gutman for "pocket money" to escort him and his team. "They wanted $400 for the escorted trip. And quite frankly, that's not much money at all per day. But I have to think three times before I spend $400 on a one-day escort into some places where there isn't that much risk ... [But] you have to pay them, because these guys are totally broke. They've got no money" (ibid.).

Although PC10 has never offered gifts or "had to bribe a rebel ... I've never thought about it or tried," she noted that small tokens given to checkpoint guards are commonplace in some regions. "[It's not only] journalists. Regular residents, they'll always give, like, cold water ... when they go through checkpoints, especially from Lebanon to Damascus" (PC10 2014).

In Afghanistan, an official refused to let one interviewee travel with his safety equipment, so "I had to pay an Afghan police officer [at the airport] to let me carry my flak jacket on a plane," he said (Interviews 2014, identity withheld).

The Camera Problem

Entrance visas are more easily obtained than permission to film, according to interviews. "Most places you can get in one way or the other. It's just whether you can get in with a camera and do your job. That's where it becomes tricky because it's one thing to be print reporter, and sometimes I pine for those days because I could just show up with a notebook and a pen. And no one knows what you're [doing]. It's pretty easy to be inconspicuous, even when you're conspicuous, and you don't look like the people there," explained Vice News' Andrew Glazer. "[But] once you have a camera, your footprint grows, and your exposure grows a lot" (Glazer 2014).

For a production in the United Arab Emirates, Glazer had applied for filming credentials through the "proper channels" in Dubai, disclosing only his general topic, not the specific subject—"Iranian money laundering." Officials approved his visa but denied his application to film. "We didn't give them explicit story subject. We just said, 'We'd like to come film. We're doing something about the relationship with Dubai and Iran'" recalled Glazer. "They didn't actually deny me access into the country. They denied me access as a journalist" (ibid.).

So Glazer arrived empty-handed, with no camera, and no camera crew, but secretly assembled a mostly local team to film. "I wound up going anyway and having a local camera crew that would film stuff outside because they had the proper credentials," he said. "We made sure we were never in the same place ever, so that if I got caught I could say, 'I'm just a tourist; I came here as a tourist … and we never got together until the very last night" (ibid.).

Throughout the entire shoot, Glazer "assumed that they know where I am … I assumed that they had my name in a database when I applied, and I got rejected, so when I went in the country, I assume all these things, although they may not be that sophisticated," he said, adding that for "most countries, you can get in, aside from North Korea" (ibid.).

Glazer is right that journalists have rarely cracked the code of North Korea, a country that has essentially sealed its borders to them, vexing long-time foreign correspondents, including Parks, who said he tried "a lot of times," but had "never gotten a visa to North Korea" (Parks 2014).

One team—from Vice News—did succeed. It was the brainchild of its Editor-in-Chief, Jason Mojica, who opened the doors through a combination of patience, persuasion, and a winning idea.

Ideas and Patience

Mojica began with the notion that "there was no chance that we were going to get into North Korea." It was part of his practice of long-range planning for multiple "pie-in-the-sky" documentaries. Because Vice News had previously produced documentaries that criticized or "made a great deal of fun of [North Korea]," featuring North Korean defectors or exposing North Korean labor camps in Far East Russia, "it didn't seem like we were an organization that they were going to welcome" (Mojica 2014).

But a combination of "two things" opened the doors. First, Mojica said, "We did ask, and we were very patient," waiting and negotiating for nearly a year. But perhaps the second factor clinched the deal. "We conjured up this idea of basketball diplomacy, knowing that Kim Jong Il, the father, was a big Chicago Bulls fan … So what we had pitched was, 'We want to engage in this sports diplomacy, this unique collaboration of sports diplomacy, and we want to make a film about it.' And that was what we said we wanted to do. And eventually, through many meetings and arm-twisting," the North Koreans let them in (ibid.).

The rare concession came with tight controls. It was the "most complicated" and "most stressful" production that Mojica had encountered. "They were controlling every minute of every day. We had to have lengthy explanations of why we needed to have exterior shots of the hotel, and there was a two-day debate. At the end of the second day, they finally let us go across the street and put a tripod there to do a tilt and a pan. And then we were like, 'Thank you.' And that was two days" (ibid.).

The restrictions exasperated the Vice News producers, so much so that "I really wanted to be at a dirty place with [just] a camera and a guy," admitted Mojica. "I was actually planning on doing a story in Syria with David Enders, and it was scheduled to be right after North Korea. And I couldn't wait for the North Korea thing to be over, so that I could go to the war-zone, just David Enders and I [sic], just a camera and him and no celebrities and their handlers and globetrotters and executives and minders" (ibid.).

Throughout the shoot, fears of worst case scenarios crept into their minds. "You had to kind of keep reminding yourself that although everything was great right now, it could suddenly turn," particularly "in a country where people get put in jail or executed for allowing dust to be on the portrait of the dear leader" (ibid.).

One potential disaster arose "the morning after the big game" when "we met Kim Jong Un … We're having lunch, and some people bring in copies of … the national newspaper, the state-run paper. And there's photos of Dennis [Rodman] and Kim Jong Un on the cover. They bring it over to Rodman. And he takes it and assumes that they want an autograph. So he takes out his pen and he just scrawls all over the picture, like signing them. And the hotel staff are freaking out because he's basically defacing the image of Kim Jong Un. They're freaking out. They don't know what to do, that they're present while this is happening. So it was like, 'We're going to get killed over this stupid shit … They're going to take our footage. They're going to erase it all, like this whole thing never existed. At the bare minimum, it's all going to be erased'" (ibid.).

Their footage survived. And no one from the production went to jail.

Instead of challenging the spin and tight controls by the North Koreans, the Vice News producers featured them as part of the story, "bringing it out to the point where it becomes obvious and sometimes funny," said Mojica. "[It] points out the absurdity and the lengths to which they are trying to spin, and that's a story in itself. It's obvious that they're spinning, and you contextualize it. You're not a mouthpiece for them. We're not transcribers. But what they're saying or showing us is absurd to the point of mockery [and] I think we can mock it by showing it. Sometimes you don't even need to make a joke out of it. It tells itself" (ibid.).

The Big Chill

Abductions, murders, imprisonment, and post-story punishment, real-life and career hazards, constrain journalistic freedom on two fronts—by removing or disabling recalcitrant journalists after the fact and by discouraging their pursuits for fear of retribution. "[If] somebody doesn't like what you write, they can throw you out. They could beat you up," said Michael Parks who has been banned or expelled from Vietnam, Libya, and Ethiopia (Parks 2014).

Parks's banishment from Vietnam resulted not from his own stories but rather "what a colleague had written," he said. "Three of us were going in together. We all got a promise of visas. We agreed on the date. This colleague, working for [*Der*] *Spiegel*, went in early and wrote things about Vietnam that were so critical, to use that word, that the Chinese military paper published them as propaganda against Vietnam. Well, our visas, which had been arranged with some Soviet help, were promptly withdrawn" (ibid.).

In Ethiopia, Parks was "expelled or escorted to the airport every time" and "even arrested." And in Libya, the government deported him after "they figured out I had gotten in ... Libya and Egypt were having a small border war, and you could cover it from the Egyptian side but not from the Libyan side. So I got on an airplane to Tripoli, and got out of the airport, had the visa stamped ... and went around and talked to the diplomats, went to a couple of hospitals. And they found me. They found me back at the American embassy. They took me out to the airport, put me back on the same plane, which had sat on the tarmac" (ibid.).

Parks was also expelled from South Africa based on his coverage of the State of Emergency and the "resistance to apartheid," he said. South African officials complained to Parks's employer and "tried to get the paper to withdraw me, which the paper did not do—the *Los Angeles Times* ... The government thought and told my editor that I was a communist agent" (ibid.).

After his expulsion, however, Parks and the *Times* managed to reverse the decision. "[We] secured a hearing [and] worked to persuade the government that it was wrong, and in the end, [we] succeeded" (ibid.).

Expelling journalists is common punishment in countries like China, according to David Schlesinger. "If they don't like what you've written, then they'll either throw you out or make your life difficult or call you in and yell at you. Or in the cases of what you see now with Bloomberg and *The New York Times*, they'll control visa access for replacements for the bureau. So Bloomberg's bureau in China has been really whittled down because they just haven't been able to bring people in" (Schlesinger 2014).

These types of sanctions constrain freedoms by putting journalists and their managers on notice, for fear of losing future needed access. "There are major journalistic organizations, [which] are based in places where they just don't go after some of the issues that they could. One example would be because of Thailand's Lèse majesté. They report that from outside, not inside. And still they're very careful about it," explained Schlesinger. "What you see in Thailand perhaps, is really getting in the way of getting the story" (ibid.).

Other countries use domestic laws to silence criticism. Singapore, for example, "doesn't censor, doesn't at all. But they are very aggressive about using the courts to go after any stories that they think are libelous or that they think violate their standards. They'll use the court system to get a financial punishment against news organizations. I think that obviously causes people to think twice," said Schlesinger. "Every country has different standards. British libel laws, which I guess you have in New Zealand, that same tradition is much stronger than US libel law. So journalists who come from Commonwealth countries are used to a different standard of caution in their writing about certain things than American journalists" (ibid.).

Still, Schlesinger warned against self-censorship, which he calls "very insidious and dangerous." But he simultaneously suggested that journalists think twice about what they write or broadcast. "Weigh the importance of a story versus the risk of that story" because "you don't want to blow your access for a story that's not worth it ... what the value of it is to your reader? It's never a binary decision, yes or no. It's a discussion about: Are there ways of doing it which can protect you? Are there ways of doing it that can protect your sources better? Are there ways of writing it that won't cause an issue?" (ibid.).

Parks agreed with the need for this type of deliberation to continue reporting. "That's not self-censorship. It's really anticipation of what the government or other actors will do" (Parks 2014).

Verification

Access is no guarantee of accuracy, and for a variety of reasons, interviewees admit the difficulty of verification under conflict conditions, including limited time in the field. For example, during Sri Lanka's civil war, McCarthy and his colleagues struggled "to work out what'd happened in certain towns and villages in the north and the east," he said. "The Tamil Tigers were attacking the government forces, and lots of people were being killed." But while trying to gather information, their "car got shot at by a helicopter … they started attacking us with 50 calibers … There was what I can only assume was an innocent farmer [who] got hit in the leg, and 50 caliber rounds are very large, and one round basically took his leg off, and nothing much we could do. We had to get out of there because the helicopters were circling" (McCarthy 2014).

Journalists are also too often "at the mercy of sources," admitted interviewees, including Parks, who recalled a colleague's remark: "I've been told a lot of lies, and I've printed most of them," but Parks added, "I like to think I stopped a lot [of lies]" (Parks 2014).

Shy of blatant lies, witnesses' memories can falter, especially after traumatic experiences. "When people are exposed to trauma, the first things out of their mouths are not necessarily accurate," explained McCarthy. "It's not that they're trying to lie to you; it's just that they're in shock and they'll say, 'oh yeah, it was awful, this person came and did this and that.' And well, maybe it wasn't exactly what happened, but it's what they'll come out with first" (McCarthy 2014).

Trauma is one obstacle of accuracy; fear of reprisals is another. "People in the United States forget this, but in a lot of countries, people are afraid of the government and afraid of what might happen to them if they just tell the truth," explained McCarthy, who encountered this type of dynamic in Cambodia and China. "There was an ongoing conflict between the Khmer Rouge guerillas and the government, which was backed by the Vietnamese. And we would go to villages, and it was quite clear that there was significant Khmer Rouge infiltration, and [its] supporters in these various villages. But they didn't want to say that in public, because they knew that the journalists were always with government guides. And so it was difficult to work out what was going on" (ibid.).

In China "they have very strong views about the government, but they're very wary about sharing those views with foreigners because they know that could get them into trouble" (ibid.).

In these cases, McCarthy sought to "somehow work the system where you had an interpreter [who] you trusted who could get away from the government guides and get some real information. If you're kind of naïve about that, you'll fly into some situation, and you'll have your guide with you who may or may not be officially working for the government but may carry some stigmas, at least as far as the locals are concerned, and you ask a question, and they'll give you a reply, which is not what they think is true, but what they think is not what will get them in trouble. And if you print that at face value, you're actually giving a misleading view of what's going on" (ibid.).

Conflicts are rife with misinformation traps, according to Gold. "Everyone's got their side and their spin and the propaganda," he said. "There's so much bullshit that's out there ... especially with young men, there's a lot of bravado. And a lot of people ... [such as] the Kurds will tell you Turkey is responsible for assassinating [someone]" (Gold 2014).

Gold relies upon his instinct, logic, the two-source rule, and the fact-checkers at his media organization to eliminate "complete bullshit; it's irresponsible to print it," he said. "So I'll edit it out, so there's a judgment call a lot of times. You can't repeat something that someone's told you once," he said. "You've got to check with other people, and if you keep hearing it over and over, and it sounds like maybe it's feasible, then you say 'claims so and so,' ... you qualify it as much as you possibly can" (ibid.).

Parks, too, warned against getting "caught up in single-source stories," which he admits are "sometimes inevitable. You [can] get caught up in somebody's biased framing of the story," he said, recalling a story he wrote in Saigon, "which was on the front page. And it was field officers saying we're pulling back out of Cambodia with most of the things not done. Can't call it a failure because they accomplished some things, but most things were not done. That was absolutely contrary to what the briefer was saying" (Parks 2014).

Vital in these cases, he said, is thorough research: "Chat with somebody else. Go to records. Chat with the opposition, if you can. Get as knowledgeable as you can, so you can detect bullshit" (ibid.).

Glazer maintains a hefty dose of skepticism, arguing that, "You don't believe a word that anyone says no matter who they are. You verify everything. I can't think of any story where I've relied on one or I needed one person, particularly an official in a place where I knew they had a reason to lie," he said. "It's not a story I would choose to do based on one person's statement" (Glazer 2014).

His media company, Vice News, avoids broadcasting elite statements altogether, according to Mojica, instead opting for "something that doesn't require that in order to make a story and probably doesn't even think to go chasing those statements" such as "things that are happening in front of our cameras" (Mojica 2014).

Direct observations are one key to distinguishing truth from bravado or propaganda in a way that interviews alone cannot. "Everybody's sort of pushing their line, or their own propaganda, which is why it is so important to be there" at the site of conflict, explained PC10. "People can tell you, 'this is happening,' but then when you are sitting there and you hear them talk and chatting, you see other things going on. I mean, I'm not somebody who gets that without actually being there" (PC10 2014).

In Libya, for example, PC10 recalled "all this bravado" voiced by the rebels during interviews. "They've [rebels] always [claimed that] the fear barrier has been broken. You heard this so much." But contradictory information emerged during downtime when they more readily discussed their true emotions, "talking about how fearful they are ... but they don't want to tell anybody because they didn't want to get [other] people afraid," she said. "Underneath this bravado, there's a lot of this fear ... but nobody's going to [say] 'I'm actually really scared.' But when you are ... overhearing their conversations ... [you understand] that's how things are." That human dimension became the focus of a Libyan conflict story, "how underneath this bravado there's a lot of this fear" (ibid.).

During the first Gulf War, a bomb exploded in an air raid shelter where "hundreds of women and children" had sought refuge. "All but a handful were killed straight away," recalled Allan Little. Combatants used the incident as part of their rhetorical war, disseminating different numbers and narratives about the death toll from the blast. "The Iraqis were saying 1,100 [civilians died]. And the allies were saying none, [alleging] 'there were no civilians in there, that it was a military command bunker'" (Little 2015).

Resolving the dispute required Little and his colleague, Marie Colvin (later killed in Syria) to physically count the bodies. "Marie and I went to the morgue together and we counted 311 women and children dead ... We got to 311, and then we got to this big pile of bodies that seemed to be fused together, and we stopped counting after that ... But at least I could say, I was able to tell you for sure that at least 300 are dead. I counted them—1, 2, 3, 4, 5, and so on. So let that be an end to the dispute" (ibid.).

Correspondents who fail to fact-check in this way abrogate their responsibility, added Little. "What you end up saying is, 'On one hand, the Iraqis say there were 1,100, but on the other, the Allies say,' and what you're saying to the audiences is, 'You pick which one you want to believe' ... That's no good really. You've got a responsibility. I mean if you go into a bar and two men are arguing, one's arguing with great conviction that two plus two equals four, and the other one is arguing with equal conviction that two plus two equals six. It's never right to say the truth lies somewhere in between. What you say is, 'The quality of evidence upon which the first one is based is quite different to the quality of evidence upon which the second one is based'" (ibid.).

The war in Sierra Leone was another case of sorting reality from rhetoric. After the British government brokered the Lomé Peace Agreement, the accord crumbled when rebels returned to fight against a weakened and disarmed government. "They [the rebels] were unsatisfied with the way they were being treated in government. And they went back to war ... The government didn't have an army to defend the populations scattered round the country, and particularly Freetown, and the United Nations fell apart. The United Nations proved itself incapable. The UN force was absolutely hopeless" (ibid.).

Britain announced the deployment of some 800 paratroopers to "evacuate British citizens and other third country nationals," he recalled.

But Little's observations contradicted the government's stated mission, which was repeated "in Parliament several times, day after day ... What I couldn't understand was why the politicians in London were saying one thing while you could see on the ground that the opposite was true. I kept saying on the air, night after night, 'Nobody here now pretends that this is about the evacuation of British people. This is not about the evacuation anymore. Britain is intervening in this civil war to try to bring about the end of the war, not by keeping the peace, but to end the war by defeating the enemy'" (ibid.).

The answers became clear when "the Brigadier who was in charge of it saw very quickly that there was an opportunity with the military personnel he had, to stop the war ... He defied orders, took a big risk with his own reputation and career. And he's told the story many times himself, so it's all on the record. So he intervened in the war. And it was an almost immediate success. It took about eight days, and he turned around the rebel advance and brought peace to the country, after which, the British government led by Tony Blair, took credit for it" (ibid.).

Little believes that "by taking sides, Britain intervened in that war, not as peacekeepers" in "a very unusual set of circumstances," which along with the "intervention in Kosovo ... helped create in the minds of Tony Blair and his colleagues, who were new to government—remember, they'd only been in power three years—an appetite for armed conflict or armed intervention that helped lead them into Afghanistan and Iraq" (ibid.).

It was New Zealand's role in the Afghanistan war that Jon Stephenson sought to fact-check, particularly after a member of the country's Special Forces was killed during a raid there. "They took the unusual step of talking about what had happened in some detail while providing their account of what happened," he said. "We hear about these things, if we hear about them at all, in a very opaque sort of manner ... But no one knew anything about it. It was completely covered up. It wasn't until a year later that some details leaked out almost by accident. And the Defense Minister, during an interview on television, was confronted with the question ... 'Did this involve the SAS?' ... And he essentially confirmed, but very few details were given" (Stephenson 2014).

That's what sent Stephenson into Afghanistan where he found the village and interviewed witnesses. "It took me quite a while to find out from sources the location of the village. And the village was in an area that was very risky to travel to. So I ended up going to meet people from the village, because civilians died in that operation," he said. "I got a very different story from the one that had been presented in the media or presented by the Defense Forces, the scripted version" (ibid.).

As detailed in Chapter 2, "On the Origin of Stories," when Gutman could not physically witness the Omarska prison camp, he sought interviews with "everybody who should know something about it, including the Serbian government," he said. "You have to go to the other side and get their explanation. And then you have to go back to the first side. And you have to go back and forth until you're convinced" (Gutman 2014).

Admittedly, "No story is perfect when you don't have total knowledge. So I don't claim it, but the story was correct about what was going on there and what was happening," he said. "I tried very hard to remember to understate things rather than overstate them … If you get proven wrong on even a detail, you're screwed as a reporter" (ibid.).

Translations also need checking. "There's been plenty of stories about how whoever you are interviewing talks for three minutes and suddenly the translator interprets the whole thing in about five seconds and then you realize, 'Wait a minute he didn't just repeat it. He just didn't translate everything,'" according to ABC broadcaster Bob Woodruff. "If we have a piece and we shoot it, we won't rely only on the translator that's with us. We find another one to translate it once we get the transcription done. We feed the tape in to New York or wherever it may be. So in most cases, we get a second opinion … The great thing is all of ours is recorded on camera, so it's easy to prove what is right or wrong" (Woodruff 2014).

As a final check, most major news organizations use layered editorial processes designed to catch misinformation. "I remember working at the [*Wall Street*] *Journal*; it went through six different people before they'd print it. They don't fuck around with fact-checking there. At *The* [*New York*] *Times* too. [But] with video, it's a little harder," Gold conceded (2014).

Journalistic Independence

Traditionally, "the value of a journalist generally is his or her independence, the autonomy of judgment," Parks said. But often, independence is lost, particularly when reporting conflict. "Typically, journalists come to identify with the institutions they cover," he said, and they "lose that autonomy either because you are reflecting on the institution report, acting as its megaphone, or perhaps the contrary, you are very hostile to a government that the United States is critical of … Pentagon correspondents can tend to think of themselves as colonels and generals" (Parks 2014).

Parks recounted one lapse during the Vietnam War when a US-based Associated Press (AP) reporter who, while "on one of the Kissinger shuttles after the '73 war, there at a briefing of the King David," asked, "'What's our position on this?' I didn't know that the AP had positions" (ibid.).

Little similarly observed journalists sounding "like spokespeople for the units that they were traveling with. They started reporting in the first person plural: 'We advanced; our tanks did this; our forces did that; we came under sustained attack; we broke through,' all this kind of thing. It made me very uncomfortable because we lost the habit of distance, or [there was] the danger, that we would lose the habit of distance, of putting distance between ourselves and one of the parties to the conflict and start identifying too emotionally, too clearly, and too explicitly with one side in the conflict, albeit the side representing the country where we came from" (Little 2015).

More recently, during the Egyptian revolution, Parks heard a Los Angeles broadcaster wishing "good luck to the people in the square in Cairo ... being very enthusiastic, [saying] 'We're changing the world' ... I was not sorry to see her move on to another position" (Parks 2014).

John Dinges is critical of journalists, such as Judith Miller of *The New York Times*, before the 2003 Iraq War, who were "so immersed in the people that were designing the policy that they saw themselves as just interpreting US policy ... It's not that they necessarily agreed with the US policy in Iraq, but they became part of it ... She [Miller] said it. I have the quote. I used it in speeches for a while. She said, 'It wasn't my job to criticize ... That wasn't my job to investigate that. My job was to describe accurately what the administration was thinking'" (Dinges 2014).

Dilemmas also arise when journalists embed with militaries and naturally develop sympathies that hamper journalistic independence.

Embedding and Censorship

Interviewees acknowledged that alongside protection and access gained by embedding with rebels or officials come tradeoffs that diminish journalistic freedoms. "There are certain rules when you embed with a military organization. You sign papers to the effect that you say you're going to respect the rules of operation and security. There are certain things that you cannot report, certain constraints in these situations," explained Balint Szlanko (2014).

The restrictions that come with embedding fell into one of two kinds of "regime control" over journalists, according to Little. During the Iraq War, for example, "You could either go and be embedded with the British or American troops ... or you could report the war from the Iraqi side," he said. "[For] those of us who reported from the Iraqi side, the censorship kicked in much earlier in terms of what we were allowed to see and hear. And everywhere we went, we had an Iraqi government minder with us, and so everybody knew they had to be careful about what they said. So by the time it came to putting our pieces together, there wasn't much. We didn't have to run our strips past an Iraqi censor. We didn't have to get permission to run this or that. The restrictions of what we could report were quite small" (Little 2015).

Journalists who embedded with the Allies, however, "got to see quite a lot and hear quite a lot and so knew quite a lot about what was going on and what was being planned. But the censorship kicked in toward the end of the reporting process, which is to say, they had to run everything past the military censor" (ibid.).

Carol Williams embedded with the US military in the 2003 Iraq War, where she faced both kinds of "regime control," even on seemingly innocuous stories. "They [the military minders] hover. We couldn't go to the bathroom without an escort. I'm not kidding," she said. "The PAO [public affairs officer], the eagle-eyed censor, they had imported all these people from Washington to be one-on-one with the journalists. It was like they just clothed you like a bad smell" (Williams 2014).

Restless with a dearth of news in the days before the invasion, Williams found a "fascinating" story when she "sat next to the ship's medical officer one night at dinner," she said. "He casually, apropos of nothing, starts talking about how, 'this is about the time when the pregnancies start showing up, because 11% of the 5,500 troops on the aircraft carrier were women. And there's a policy that you can't be serving on a warship if you are pregnant … He was saying that they had to medevac a woman off the ship because she was pregnant, and I was thinking, 'There's like, wow, there's pregnant women? How did they get pregnant? Isn't there an anti-fraternization policy here?' And he said, 'Yeah, but we have an average of 20 pregnancies per deployment'" (ibid.).

Williams pursued the story but was quickly admonished by the PAO. "The admiral told the PAO that I was NOT to write this story," she recalled. "He and I were just at loggerheads for days over this, and finally … he just told me I couldn't write it, and I did … I had very bad relations with the PAO by the time I got off that ship" (ibid.).

In the end, Williams reported both the story and the struggle over the story in the *Los Angeles Times*. "I wrote this story about the war over whether I could write the fraternization," she said. "The funny thing was that the army and the marines, they came out looking really good because they were both being very helpful to their embedded reporters, but the navy was just in such control-freak mode they came off looking hysterical" (ibid.).

Stephenson also embedded with the US military after a period of reporting unilaterally, but he said "None of that happened to me. I mean, obviously, they had the power of deciding where you go and so on. But that unit that I was with, they were under so much pressure. I mean, you were sleeping in the same rooms as they were. You were going on the same patrols as they were. You were experiencing pretty much the same risks as they were. The only difference is you didn't have a weapon and you weren't engaged in the fighting," he said. "Some of these guys, they were shooting civilians, sometimes by mistake; and they would come back, and they'll tell you, 'oh I shot this guy by mistake today,' … or 'my friend got his legs blown off,' … or whatever it was. And they couldn't put up sort of a front in the way you might do at a safer location where you get these briefings. So it was much more raw and just being with them all that time" (Stephenson 2014).

But Stephenson admitted the sympathies that he developed for the soldiers. He had expected "not to like them … And I'd be lying if I said that I didn't like these guys. A lot of them are really nice people … They were basically pretty decent guys, I can honestly say" (ibid.).

Stephenson's experience illuminated a subconscious influence. "I saw the dangers of embedding as not being that they control everything you do, and try and stop you writing this or that, but that it's like [we're] going to a dangerous area, and someone picks you up at the airport. They take you to the house. They are providing security for you. They are providing food … And they are protecting you from the bad guys. It's very hard to turn around and [criticize them]" (ibid.).

Glazer concurred, arguing that "eventually, yes, you are going to be sympathetic to the people who are protecting your life, so I think it's a good question to ask. And I don't think it's really being asked that much anymore. It's become pretty conventional to embed" (Glazer 2014).

Circumventing Direct Censorship

Successful negotiation of access and gifted production or prose still do not guarantee a story's survival. For example, "the democratic, Jewish state in the Middle East, Israel, has active censorship to which foreign correspondents are obliged, if asked, to show their copy, [to] clear their copy," said Parks. "As I think about it, that's the primary place that my stories were subject to state censorship pre-publication censorship. There was censorship of some sort in Cambodia. And there was censorship of some sort in Laos. This was in the '70s … They imposed censorship" (Parks 2014).

With some persuasion, Parks managed to clear his stories in Israel. The censor had rejected one Parks story about the "military's planned use of self-propelled howitzers," on grounds of being too "dangerous," he recalled. So Parks persuaded the military spokesman to help him get approval. "I said 'Talk to the censor. You showed us this. I've written about it. If you didn't want us to write about it, why did you take us there? And by the way it's all on film, and it's going out on the evening flights.'" Eventually the censors relented (ibid.).

Another article designated for the trash-bin covered sexual harassment in Israel's military of its female soldiers. "The censor did not like it because there were no official spokesmen in the story," an easy fix, according to Parks. "I called up and got a spokesman to say '[sexual harassment] doesn't happen,' [although] it was quite clear that the comeliest of the young Israeli women were assigned to the offices of the most senior generals, those young women who were trained as instructors. Interesting to me was that many of the women who served in the IDF (Israel Defense Forces) were instructors for the male recruits … The instructors were women, even though they wouldn't go into battle" (ibid.).

Journalists circumvent censors, sometimes simply by ignoring them. Stephenson, for example, traveled to Gaza three times as both a print and television journalist. By obligation, he signed forms, agreeing to submit his stories through the government clearance process. But "we just do our stuff and send it. We never got it approved" (Stephenson 2014).

Stephenson believes that Israel's censors relented because of his country's size. "I think your treatment in Israel is in inverse proportions to, number one, the amount of people that you are reaching," he said. "So if you are from the United States, and you're giving bad criticism, serious criticism, then you can expect [censorship], or Britain ... you will come under a lot of pressure, whether it's from the pro-Israeli lobby groups or the government itself, or people in your own country. But here [in New Zealand], there is a very small Jewish community ... [and] New Zealand's not the frontline" (ibid.).

Other governments had tried and failed to censor foreign correspondents. "The South Africans ... found it such a cumbersome process that they just kind of abandoned it [censorship efforts]," said Parks. "The first time I was in Egypt, after the '73 war, they had official censorship, but you couldn't find the censors ... So the hell with it. The Israelis in that period were still imposing censorship. And the censorship regulations, I should point out, are under British colonial regulations" (Parks 2014).

Parks believes that censorship may have met its match with the internet, "In the digital era, [censorship] it's become rather harder to exercise," he said. "But [in Israel] your copy is still monitored. And Israel is quite capable of doing that. They're quite capable of listening to phone conversations, and [they] do. And if you know that there's something in your copy that needs to be cleared, you're obliged to get approval from the censor. They have tremendous language capability; they can read almost anything" (ibid.).

The Cutting Room at Home

Terry McCarthy and his CBS News team embedded with a US Marine battalion for most of a year, first filming their training in the US, then into Afghanistan, where they forcibly took a village from the Taliban and began clearing bombs from the area. "We were pretty much part of their family, and then we came back with them. And we got to know a bunch of them pretty well" (McCarthy 2014).

While in Afghanistan, the broadcasters followed "[a marine] using robots to investigate suspect devices and pulling wires out of the ground and blowing up bombs that were too dangerous to touch and so on," McCarthy said. "Over a period of two weeks, they had pulled out some 400 bombs" (ibid.).

On "day seven," however, the marine ostensibly "had a momentary lapse; his metal detector was lifted or something" (ibid.). The error proved fatal. "He put his foot on a bomb, blew himself up. It blew his legs off, threw him up in the air, and he came back down on his back," recalled McCarthy. "The guy next to him got the blast in his head. It took the top of his skull off. His brains were hanging out, and he basically was dead on arrival ... They kept him alive until they got him to Germany, flew his family from the States, but he was on a machine; he wasn't conscious, and then they turned the machine off, and he was ... he expired" (ibid.).

The battalion's commander came to the side of the first Marine. "He [the Marine] knew that his legs were gone, and he was unable to see temporarily [because] the soft tissue round his eyes swelled up because he took some shrapnel in the face," said McCarthy. "And Johnny said, the first words out of his mouth [were], 'I'm sorry, I screwed up, sir.' That's real. That's why I told the story. It's a real butt-grabber. You know, it's a marine. They're tough, responsible people" (ibid.).

McCarthy and his team caught the entire series of events on tape but pixelated the graphic images to soften the gore, only to have the segment rejected by their executive producer. "We have this footage, and CBS news, their executive producer, I'm ashamed to say, didn't want to show it. I was shocked," said McCarthy. "And the ostensible reason was it was too gruesome for our viewers. And we had pixelated it so you didn't actually see the brains and the blood, but it was clear what had happened" (ibid.).

McCarthy believes the decision was profit-motivated. "The real reason, I think, was that it was too gruesome for the advertisers. That's always the problem with war. And CNN has that problem. Their ratings go up when there's a war, but the advertising goes down" (ibid.).

Eventually, McCarthy won the argument on the basis "that it's the media's duty to show the costs of war," he said. "I have, for a long time, been very unsatisfied with the US media in the way it does not show American casualties. We see lots of pictures of dead Taliban and dead Iraqis and dead Al Qaeda, but they don't show American casualties. And I understand there are privacy issues here, but nonetheless, we're fighting a war and to give the impression that Americans aren't touched by this is fundamentally dishonest" (ibid.).

The series won an Emmy Award, which McCarthy believes was "because so few other networks or media outlets of any type were prepared to show American casualties. It's not that common," he said. "If you recall, early on in the Iraq War, they wouldn't even allow the media to show returning coffins ... That's insane. I mean, these are wooden boxes with the American flag on them. There's nothing you can say that that is in any way gruesome or intrusive" (ibid.).

Editorial sanitizing of images is not necessarily unusual. During the Iraq War, "There were multiple times when ... photographers would've had pictures that their editors said, 'well we can't show that.' And yet, when there's an Iraqi ... I remember there was a famous case of an unfortunate young boy. He was 12, young guy, in the early days of the invasion in 2003, who was burnt severely by some hostile activity," said McCarthy. "He ended up in American hands and *Time* magazine ran a picture of him, and he was scarred, looked like something that had come off a barbecue. It was atrocious, very gruesome, and *Time* magazine ran it, and then there was this push to get him sent to the United States. And readers of the magazine said, 'We will finance his cosmetic surgery,' and that's what happened. And he was sent to the US. He was given the best surgery the United States has to offer. But he was an Iraqi, so the argument that things are too gruesome to show I think doesn't bear up. It's clearly not the case ... It's more [that] we don't want to show American casualties and I think that's wrong" (ibid.).

Many interviewees faced similar professional frustrations; so much so that framing to persuade editors and executives became key parts of their jobs. Gutman faced delays and rejections, both on his proposed coverage of the former Yugoslavia and his more recent stories from Syria. "I've got stories that are sitting on my editor's desk right now that have been there for months that would reveal at least the reporting of how Assad helped this jihadist movement take root and thrive in Syria ... And why? Because the editor says, 'Nobody else has done this story,' and, 'Aren't you taking people's word for things?' and, 'What about the other side?'" (Gutman 2014).

The experience mirrored another time when Gutman predicted the "coming war in Bosnia," he said. "At one point I went to the editors at *Newsday* and I said, 'look, I've got one of the biggest stories I've ever seen, and it's starting in Croatia, but it's going to blow up the whole Balkan region, and it could blow up Europe.' And they all sort of said, 'Why don't you do something else?'" (ibid.).

In the latter case, Gutman believed his editors were "wary of a predictive story ... the coming war in Bosnia. But he persisted. "They sat on that story for six weeks. And I had to rewrite it four or five times, and the last one was on Christmas Eve when there was a peg, when there was a better peg," he explained. "And I think the editors felt guilty. I had really great editors there. But even great editors are wary of a predictive story. And that took me six weeks" (ibid.).

Little had a similar clash with editors when reporting from the former Yugoslavia. As Little said in Chapter Two, "I wrote a piece in 1993, which was never broadcast, saying, 'When Srebrenica falls, whether it's next week or next month or next year, and hundreds of men are taken into a field and shot, and buried in mass graves—when that happens, let none of us say we didn't know. Because we do know.' And it wasn't broadcast. My editor back in London thought it was intemperate and partisan" (Little 2015).

Language was also a "continual fight" for Little. "I would always say 'the Bosnian government forces, the Bosnian government side,' whereas they wanted to say 'Muslim forces.' And that made the Bosnian government side, in a sense, morally equivalent to the Serb nationalists and the

Croat nationalists because if it was really a straightforward tribal war between three people of irreconcilable ethnic differences, then it's very easy to deal with," he recalled. "To me it was a three-sided war in which two sides represented some sort of ethnic supremacy, and the idea of ethnic exclusivity and pursued that through means of ethnic cleansing. And the third side represented approximating to mainstream European values, which was to say multi-ethnic tolerance means tolerance and so on. Then you can't so easily impose a moral equivalent. So [my editor] called them 'the Muslims,' and so on [as if] they're all the same [as the Serbs and the Croats]. But I didn't think they were all the same. I thought they represented fundamentally different sorts of values" (ibid.).

Routine decisions to censor, kill, or soften stories can sometimes cause journalists to suppress their own instincts in anticipation of their editors' sensibilities. But others fight for their stories. Gutman's formula is to "be ahead" but not "too far ahead of your time in doing a story ... Events will prove you right. So in other words, never give up. Don't walk away from something. Stick to your guns. Find another way to tell it" (Gutman 2014).

For example, he found stories from war-zones hard to sell because they "really cause eyes to glaze over after the first few days because nobody really can tell one from another, and the politics sound too complex" (ibid.).

His remedy was "to package stories. And I could do this at *Newsday* because it fit their format a lot, which was, you've got to have photographs to back up your text. You've got to have a strong narrative in the text. You've got to have real people. You've got to tell two stories in the package: One hard news, one sort of feature-y. This may sound like an abstract exercise, but I'm convinced that it works. Nothing can work as well as that because it gives different aspects to a reader, and if they're going to follow it up, and that will convince them on day one that there's really a story" (ibid.).

In Syria, however, Gutman admits that the "old formula that I used before is not working here—our man on the scene goes out and finds the story and people read and they react," said Gutman. "The whole world has turned away from it. And yet it contains the seeds for major disasters in the future. If I could figure out what to do, I would do it. But I only do it story by story, so what I'm doing now is I'm tracking ... We need to rethink what we're doing in order to make it effective" (ibid.).

Because Gold pursues lesser known subjects, he strategically frames them to relate to visceral or newsy topics. For example, on its face, Gold knew his story, about "the Rohingya in Burma," would not be "something that my editor has taken a particular interest in, but you have to know how to frame it" (Gold 2014).

To persuade his editor, Gold connected the issues in the democratizing country to the 2015 US presidential election. "I know Obama is visiting there in the next month, and also Burma's transition to a democracy has been Hillary's coup for the State Department. A lot of people say that the democracy is kind of bullshit. And when you have an ethnic cleansing going on, like the story that I want to cover, you know in the 2015 election lead-up, there's going to be a lot of questions about that. Obviously I don't care about how it affects her campaign, don't care at all. But if I need to frame it that way to get out in the field and cover it, you know. I wouldn't want to make my story about that. I probably won't even mention it more than two or three times, but if I've got to frame it that way to get someone to give me money to go there, then I'll do that" (ibid.).

In the end, Gold called the story "Asia's Apartheid," asserting "That's going to sell. People are going to be interested in that, apartheid in Asia" (ibid.).

A New World with New Media

Most interviewees prefer to gather their own information first-hand, leaving social media only for background research. But collective developments— increased hazards, economic constraints in media, and the emergence of citizen journalism—arising from uncertain safety and budgetary shortfalls have forced some journalists and media organizations to use these sources more frequently when they cannot access the region of interest. For example, "there was not a lot of Western media in Iran" during the so-called Green Revolution in Iran, leading media companies to seek ways of covering the developments from afar, gathering and studying the videos uploaded by local Iranian residents, explained Glazer (2014).

So Glazer and his colleagues sought to "find a way to verify this stuff. And that was a big challenge, because those were the only images that were really available," he said about the Iranian videos. "When that young woman [Neda Agha-Soltan] was killed, that was an image that the Iranians were trying to discredit, and so you want to know that it's right" (Glazer 2014). Similarly, during the early days of the Syrian conflict, before the violence broke out, "it was still tough to get there," he said. "And you want to cover the war" (ibid.).

Gutman agreed that problems of verification are a reason to avoid using social media as a source. "You've got to, basically, verify things. And if things don't verify, you've got to find out why they don't verify. And then you've got to find out what the facts really are. And that's a job that takes longer than uploading a video," argued Gutman. "We have rules that editors apply, that if you don't have editors, don't get applied, like verifying your information" (Gutman 2014).

In response, new organizations, such as Storyful, that analyze and authenticate social media materials, such as YouTube videos, have emerged. "What they do all day long is try and verify the authenticity of videos," using many criteria, including, "if they've been uploaded before, if they're in some other place," explained Mojica. Typically, the companies use "standard open-source methods," asking, "Does this mountain range actually match this and that? And also doing a lot of putting it out to open-source verification is having, just making use of people online to provide information or debunk things. And so they're really good at that. That actually provides news organizations with a bit of a safety net and a cushion, basically. Of course, if you get it wrong, you're not going to be able to blame them, but you feel a lot more comfortable using them, and the tools that they use and the rigor that they put into it" (Mojica 2014).

Still, journalists such as Williams dislike using online sources, except as "imagery" or to "illustrate something that's being reported, like by *Al Jazeera.*" She, like most interviewees prefers using her own reporting along with "material from sources I can trust—AP, the BBC, Reuters ... or things that speak for themselves. When you see dead bodies on the ground and troops with markings standing victoriously over them, you know that it's pretty obvious what's going on" (Williams 2014). Still, legacy media have used unverified footage, but mostly, they qualify it with "'validity of this could not be ascertained' or some caveat," said Williams (ibid.).

Verification is not the only problem, noted interviewees. Without context, audiences cannot understand the events in any meaningful way. "It's one thing to film it, but as we know ... you can get fantastic videos of something, but the question is, what's the narration? What's the narrative? And that's where print comes in, and that's where old fashioned shoe-leather journalism comes in," remarked Gutman. "The packaging of facts is really half of our job. But if you don't spend your energies digging them out, you will be condemned to superficial reporting. You'll have a hard time ever finding judgment. You'll be at the mercy of governments and of people who manipulate the media. And I think it's very hard to get beyond that ... If you [have] editors devoted to doing nothing but vetting and editing material from that particular war-zone, we might be able to come up with real narratives and to produce the story, because enough narratives, and you've got the story ... And then the public has no excuse for not understanding it. And then in the course of doing that you'd also come up with some humdingers that would really make people pay attention" (Gutman 2014).

Syria, he said, is a perfect example, of "the profound flaws in citizen journalism, because I've heard a thousand videos a day are posted from Syria, some immense number per month. And what happens to them? They disappear because nobody trusts them. Nobody knows who the reporter is. Nobody knows whether they've really done their homework" (ibid.).

Further, because the imagery is "taken by somebody that's probably not a journalist, it might be for ulterior motives. They might be trying to promote one aspect or another of the story, and all you've got to see is what's on that tape," explained Williams. "You have no context for it. So unless it's really necessary, I try not to use unsubstantiated video or anything that's suspect, you know. You don't know what the purpose of it is" (Williams 2014).

When traditional media use the material without context, they produce the "wrong" response from the audiences, argued Glazer. "You see this, not only in conflict now, but ABC News, what they do, typically, in every broadcast now is, 'here's what's happening on social [media]. Here's the video, the viral video thing.' There's no context and that's the story, just the image itself. And particularly in contact, in combat or in conflict, the images are often titillating and sometimes they tickle the wrong part of your brain. It's not the part of your brain that says, 'God, this is awful. What's going on there?' It's, 'wow, this is exciting. There's bombs and bang-bang.' And without the eyes on the ground and the context and the reporting, you're just relying on those images. And so it can be misused ... I see that over and over again, and even in the mainstream news broadcasts, you see the story driven by a particular image. And there's not a lot of explanation or context anywhere" (Glazer 2014).

Szlanko believes that some websites, such as Brown Moses, have taken the time to verify and contextualize. "[The founder] he's basically watching these videos every day, and he's usually the first. He discovered, solely by watching these videos—he has never been to Syria—that the Saudis were arming, were sending heavy weapons to some of rebel groups in the southwest of Syria, last year or the year before that. And it was a huge story, and he got into *The New York Times* and everything" (Szlanko 2014).

Szlanko uses this and other trusted websites to learn about "places where you can't get to," but he added that "a lot of people seem to do very little but watch YouTube, trying to figure what's going on in Syria through these YouTube channels" (ibid.).

As a freelancer, Szlanko studies the videos himself, relying upon his own "common sense to try to figure out what's real and what's not," he said. "For example, a couple of days ago there was a video making the rounds on YouTube ... That shows a boy who's trying to save a girl from a sniper. And the boy gets shot, and then he stands up and tries to drag the girl into safety, and I didn't like the video because I thought the way this boy is falling after he's shot just looks unnatural ... That's not how people fall when they get shot. It looks very theatrical, and I had a hunch that it wasn't real. It was a set up. And then it later turned out that a lot of people felt the same, and they looked at the video, and they made some slow motion things, and they were there, and it can't be real" (ibid.).

Szlanko still uses social media and the web to "follow people who are better than me," such as Brown Moses. "I tend to trust his judgment ... he's got a big reputation now. He's a very capable man" (ibid.).

About one third of interviewees used Twitter for background information, using tags and alerts on their subjects as well as staying atop the most recent news. Szlanko for example spends "a bit of time on Twitter every day [to] see what's trending and what other people follow ... So if you cover Ukraine, you look at the Ukraine tag and see what's going on, see who your friends follow, so just what everybody else does really" (ibid.).

For example, Sandra Rodriguez Nieto found social media "absolutely useful" for background research on big investigations such as Mexican energy reform and for hearing from citizens about "police abuses, some shootouts, things like that," she said. But she, too, is wary of taking social media at face value. "It must have a lot of analysis. I think that's something that you learn to understand with time. In Mexico, for instance, there was a case days ago. It was a video of a shootout circulating in the media. It's not that I just got it. Everybody has it. And I was careful ... You have to analyze it to understand the context to know if those are shootouts or not" (Rodriguez Nieto 2014).

PC10 is less inclined to use social media, stating that "I don't think I've ever used [social media] to get a story." She has, however, opted to use new technology to interview people with whom she cannot meet in person. "Skype has been the main way that Western journalists have been able to cover Syria when we are not on the ground, because even the reporters who are covering Syria almost full-time spend [only] a few weeks there a year. In this past year I have spent a month inside Syria, that's it. And then other years, like last year, I think I spent maybe two weeks or something ... Covering Syria specifically has been very, very hard. So Skype has been ... the main way that I connect with people ... [By] chatting with people regularly, you know what's going on," she said. "People use Facebook and other things, but Skype has been one of the best ways to do that, and it is also seen as more secure" (PC10 2014).

Predictably, all interviewees agreed that the "best case scenario" is when they report and shoot their own images because "not only do you know that it's true but you have context. So whether it's in voice-over or it's in editing, or the way you explain stuff, it was you and your camera person and the correspondent or some combination of that who [were] there" (Glazer 2014).

References

C11. 2014. Personal Interview. In Person. New York. October 30.
Dinges, John. 2014. Personal Interview. In Person. Washington, DC. November 3.
Glazer, Andrew. 2014. Personal Interview. In Person. Brooklyn, NY. October 31.
Gold, Danny. 2014. Personal Interview. In Person. Brooklyn, NY. October 31.
Gutman, Roy. 2014. Personal Interview. Via Skype. Auckland to Istanbul. December 6.

Jamail, Dahr. 2014. Personal Interview. Via Telephone. November 10.

Little, Allan. 2015. Personal Interview. Via Telephone. Auckland to London. January 27.

McCarthy, Terry. 2014. Personal Interview. In Person. Los Angeles. July 7.

Mojica, Jason. 2014. Personal Interview. In Person. Brooklyn, NY. October 31.

Parks, Michael. 2014. Personal Interview. Los Angeles. November 18.

PC10. 2014. Personal Interview. In Person. Site withheld. November 11.

Rodriguez Nieto, Sandra. 2014. Personal Interview. Via Skype. Los Angeles to Mexico City. November 17.

Schlesinger, David. 2014. Personal Interview. Via Skype. Los Angeles to Hong Kong. November 27.

The Scholars' Circle. 2012. "Reporting from the Danger Zone." Panel discussion. First broadcast September 30.

Stephenson, Jon. 2014. Personal Interview. In Person. Auckland, NZ. December 12.

Szlanko, Balint. 2014. Personal Interview. Via Skype. November 12.

Williams, Carol. 2014. Personal Interview. In Person. Los Angeles. June 26.

Woodruff, Bob. 2014. Personal Interview. Via Telephone. Los Angeles to New York. November 13.

7 Conclusion

Words, images and their organization shape the meanings, beliefs, and emotions that impel us toward individual and collective action or inaction (Edelman 1971, 2001). In times of crisis and conflict, they can mean life or death (Armoudian 2011). War-wagers use them in as effort to win in the battlefield of hearts and minds in aid to the physical battlefield. They wage a rhetorical war—or a frame war—to convince their audiences and potential recruits of the importance or justness of their cause while they seek to persuade the enemy of their power and prowess.[1] Throughout modern history, war-makers have used mass media for these purposes and more.

Ethical journalism acts as a check on distortions, propaganda, or other falsehoods, and most interviewed journalists believed this to be a key part of their job description. Most had endured terrifying, gut-wrenching, even life-threatening ordeals in their efforts to deliver stories that they believed were important—stories of people who would have otherwise been forgotten, facts about transgressions or abuse, or to prevent a piece of truth from becoming the so-called first casualty.[2] This duty is ingrained in their professional identities and triggered by a range of humanitarian values and emotions that range from compassion and hope to outrage. Interviewees largely wanted to contribute to solving big, painful problems in the world. With similar orientations, values, and emotions, journalists—both past and present, local and foreign—chose stories primarily for one or all of three reasons—issues they wanted addressed, matters of personal interest, or information they believed their audiences needed or desired. These were the constants—across interviewees.

But just as journalism can affect the politics of life and death, the politics of life and death affects journalism. The physical and psychological wounds[3] are sometimes debilitating, mentally and physically, and can impair the once-determined journalist when hopes and expectations fade to disillusionments and disappointments. At least one interviewee had become despondent while two grew more determined. And many reported a struggle to heal their traumas. Most needed absences of various durations from the danger zones to recover from their experiences. Some recalibrated their goals from that of change-agent to a still honorable and Herculean role of recorder of history, while others had long relinquished hope that journalism offered change. As noted by Jason Mojica of Vice News, "The work transforms the worker" with a wide range of effects in attitudes, political views, in daily life, and in career options.

The risks and traumas are real. Four interviewees had been abducted, one was tortured. Many were detained, had close brushes with death, and faced ongoing threats of violence against them and their families. Psychologists and scholars have documented high rates of depression, substance abuse, PTSD and related disturbances (Feinstein 2006). And as Terry McCarthy noted, because there is no "Vets administration for journalists," health care falls onto large media companies or as is the case for freelancers and local journalists, on themselves, individually. These very real afflictions curbed the journalists' range of subjects—out of self-preservation, physically, mentally, and professionally. For local danger zone journalists, the threats seep into their everyday lives as they remain day and night in the danger zones. Worse yet, for many local journalists, stigma adds insult to injury.

There are, however, profound differences between danger zone journalism of past and present. As wars have changed, so too have approaches to journalism. The days of clear delineations between combatants and territories have faded, as have safe zones for journalists and their roles as civilians who are not to be attacked. Instead, journalists have become ammunition in the real-life "game of thrones," used by some as ransoms, or their public deaths as displays of power. As a reasonable response, media organizations have increasingly refused to subject correspondents to the possible loss of life or limb. But as a consequence, entire regions of the world go unreported, events go unknown, leaving policymakers and citizens of the world in the dark, without adequate information to appropriately respond.

There are also important differences between foreign correspondents and local journalists—in the specific subjects they pursued and in the emotional intensity they experienced. For example, while the foreign danger zone correspondent is compelled by stories of international appeal, such as large-scale human rights issues, interest in specific geographic regions, and the penchant for the excitement and travel, the local danger zone journalists are more inclined to focus on untangling and exposing local vexing issues—whether internationally appealing or not—to improve the lot for their fellow citizens: life-sustaining necessities, alongside issues such as corruption, economics, police abuse, and an end to senseless violence that upended their own communities. They often looked beyond the "news" to find solutions to big looming problems in their countries.

All interviewees expressed compassion and empathy for victims of violence, abuse, and failed institutions, and most were vicariously traumatized as a result. Yet the local journalists' work is deeply personal: It is their family, friends and neighbors who are among the fallen, their cities that are destroyed, and their countries that have come apart. For these problems, they seek solutions through their journalism, and their audiences' needs are different from those of the foreign correspondent.

The perils besetting the local danger zone journalist are proportionally greater. As foreign correspondents slip in and out of the danger zones, local journalists live there and must contend with the hazards on a daily basis, navigating physical, legal, and rhetorical battles that threaten their lives and livelihoods. A misplaced word, a misquotation can bring the wrath of the state or insurgent, or cost their jobs and sources. They cross these terrains like obstacle courses, using objectivity as more than a news norm but as a virtual shield for life or livelihood.

Foreign correspondents, however, face a different set of complications. They must gain access, often through hostile terrain, and learn—as they go—new lands, local politics, culture, and customs. And as Michael Parks noted, "access comes with rules," rules that some journalists pains-takingly follow, while others skirt by, slipping into their targeted region using stealth or charm offensives, particularly when no official visa is forth-coming. Mostly, foreign correspondents must find and retain local guides, who help with every aspect of their journalism—story leads and tips, trans-portation, translation, and safety. These local guides—or "fixers"—are one of the most important aspects of reporting and of staying alive while entering, covering, and exiting danger zones. Some fixers betrayed—intentionally or inadvertently—their correspondents.

As some regions have become entirely unsafe, the primary safety strategy was avoidance altogether. Yet some journalists still take the risk, sneaking in and blending in with the locals. Others embed with either militaries or insurgencies, to gain access to the frontlines while receiving some protection. But embedding comes with a cost, as journalists readily admitted. Strict control or censorship constrains journalistic freedom, and sympathies develop for their protectors. Journalists also face post-story punishment, which in the worst cases, can mean death, detention, deportation, or injury, depending on the time, place, and publication. It is all in the struggle over the so-called "first casualty," wresting that piece of truth from dying in obscurity.

Journalists cannot be everywhere at all times, nor all-knowing (Lippman 1922), and they are only human. Yet it is their humanity that guides their choices. So their backstories about their stories are profoundly insightful as a study of the fortitudes and frailties of humanity as well as the dynamics and struggles of the information wars,[4] revealing factors that determine the information we receive and the information we do not receive from danger zones. Safety, for example, dictates a very large part of these stories; but so, too, does the individual journalist's resourcefulness, humanitarian values, personal interests, and emotions, and of course, the structures and norms of journalism itself, the media organizations, and the political terrain.

This book adds to the great wealth of studies related to danger zone journalism which have helped us to understand the special dynamics of war reporting (Allan and Zelizer 2004; Bennett 2013; Busch 2012; Collings 2010; Feinstein 2006; Geyer 1997; Ghaffar 2005; Kellner 2008; Knightley 2002; Lisosky and Henrichsen 2009; Loyd 2001; Lynch et al. 2010; Markham 1974; Matheson and Allan 2009; McLaughlin 2002; Moorcraft and Taylor 2008; Murrell 2010; Pfau et al. 2005; Richards et al. 2011; Seib 2004; Sweeney 2006; Taylor 2011; Thussu and Freedman 2003; Tumber & Webster 2006; Williams 2012), affirming some previous findings and expanding them, examining the role of emotions, comparing past to present, and local journalist to foreign correspondent, and contextualizing these in life and death scenarios. By examining danger zone journalism as a broad category that includes war, organized crime, corruption, and authoritarian rule, we see the constants and variations across these categories.

Journalists and their work are vital for the delivery of much-needed, accurate, contextual information to local and international communities who depend on them for these truths. International organizations, including the United Nations, have begun taking actions to protect them. In May of 2015, the UN adopted Resolution 2222, which affirmed their civilian status and the importance of a free media (United Nations Resolution 2222 2015). Two years earlier, it adopted A/RES/68/163, declaring November 2 as the "International Day to End Impunity for Crimes Against Journalists," and called on member states to take action to enforce international law protecting journalists as civilians (United Nations Resolution A/RES68/163 2013). But as Reporters without Borders (Reporters sans frontières—RSF) and other organizations argue, resolutions are not meaningful without enforcement structures. RSF called for a new special representative at the UN to specifically oversee the safety of journalists. This and other proposals are important first steps in freeing information and protecting their messengers. But much more work is needed from scholars, international law experts, and journalists themselves in devising safer ways to secure vital information.

Notes

1 The terms rhetorical and frame war are mine but others refer to the phenomenon differently. Philip Seib calls this "intellectual warfare" while Liz Curtis calls it a "propaganda war."
2 The "first casualty" in war is truth, according to US Senator Hiram Johnson (Kamalipour and Snow 2004: xi). The phrase was also the title of the important book on war journalism by Phillip Knightley (2002).
3 Feinstein's *Journalists Under Fire* (2006) and Backholm and Bjorkqvist (2010) detail psychological conditions of war correspondents. This work explores these wounds in the larger contexts.
4 Also called propaganda wars (Curtis 1984), intellectual wars (Seib 2004), frame wars and rhetorical wars (Armoudian 2011).

References

Armoudian, Maria. 2011. *Kill the Messenger: The Media's Role in the Fate of the World*. Amherst, NY: Prometheus Books.

Allan, Stuart, and Barbie Zelizer. 2004. *Reporting War: Journalism in Wartime*. New York: Routledge.

Backholm, Klas, and Kaj Bjorkqvist. 2010. "The Effects of Exposure to Crisis on Well-being of Journalists: A Study of Crisis Related Factors Predicting Psychological Health in a Sample of Finnish Journalists." *Media, War & Conflict* 3(2): 138–151.

Bennett, Daniel. 2013. "Exploring the Impact of an Evolving War and Terror Blogosphere on Traditional Media Coverage of Conflict." *Media, War & Conflict* 6(1): 37–53.

Busch, Peter. 2012. "The Future of War Reporting." *The RUSI Journal* 157(3): 60–67.

Collings, Anthony. 2010. *Capturing the News: Three Decades of Reporting Crisis and Conflict*. Columbia: University of Missouri Press.

Curtis, Liz. 1984. *Ireland: The Propaganda War – The British Media and the Battle for Hearts and Minds*. London: Pluto Press.

Edelman, Murray. 1971. *Politics as Symbolic Action: Mass Arousal and Quiescence*. Chicago: Markham Publishing Company.

Edelman, Murray. 2001. *The Politics of Misinformation*. New York: Cambridge University Press.

Feinstein, Anthony. 2006. *Journalists under Fire: The Psychological Hazards of Covering War*. Baltimore: Johns Hopkins University Press.

Geyer, Georgie Anne. 1997. "The War against War Correspondents." *World and I* 12(5): 78.

Ghaffar, Omar. 2005. "Reporting under Fire: Understanding Psychopathology of War Journalists." *Psychiatric Times* 22(4): 31.

Kamalipour, Y.R. and Snow, N., 2004. *War, media, and propaganda: A global perspective*. Rowman & Littlefield.

Kellner, Douglas. 2008. "War Correspondents, the Military, and Propaganda: Some Critical Reflections." *International Journal of Communication* 2.

Knightley, Phillip. 2002. *The First Casualty: The War Correspondent as Hero and Myth-maker from the Crimea to Kosovo*. Baltimore, MD: Johns Hopkins University Press.

Lippman, Walter. 1922. *Public Opinion*. New York: The Free Press.

Lisosky, Joanne M., and Jennifer Henrichsen. 2009. "Don't Shoot the Messenger: Prospects for Protecting Journalists in Conflict Situations." *Media, War & Conflict* 2(2): 129–148.

Loyd, Anthony. 2001. *My War Gone By, I Miss It So*. New York: Penguin.

Lynch, George, Frederick Palmer, and John Maxwell Hamilton. 2010. *In Many Wars, by Many War Correspondents*. Updated edn. Baton Rouge: Louisiana State University Press.

McLaughlin, Greg. 2002. *The War Correspondent*. London; Sterling, VA: Pluto Press.

Markham, Tim. 1974. *The Politics of War Reporting Authority: Authenticity and Morality*. Manchester: Manchester University Press.

Matheson, Donald, and Stuart Allan. 2009. *Digital War Reporting*. Cambridge: Polity.

Moorcraft, Paul L., and Philip M. Taylor. 2008. *Shooting the Messenger: The Political Impact of War Reporting.* 1st edn. Washington, DC: Potomac Books.

Murrell, Colleen. 2010. "Baghdad Bureaux: An Exploration of the Interconnected World of Fixers and Correspondents at the BBC and CNN." *Media, War & Conflict* 3(2): 125–137.

Pfau, Michael, Elaine M. Wittenberg, Carolyn Jackson, Phil Mehringer, Rob Lanier, Michael Hatfield, and Kristina Brockman. 2005. "Embedding Journalists in Military Combat Units: How Embedding Alters Television News Stories." *Mass Communication and Society* 8(3): 179–195.

Richards, Amy, and Jolyon Mitchell. 2011. "Journalists as Witnesses to Violence and Suffering." In Robert S. Fortner and P. Mark Fackler (eds) *The Handbook of Global Communication and Media Ethics* vol. 2, chapter 38. Oxford: Wiley-Blackwell.

Seib, Philip M. 2004. *Beyond the Front Lines: How the News Media Cover a World Shaped by War.* New York: Palgrave Macmillan.

Sweeney, Michael. 2006. *The Military and the Press: An Uneasy Truce.* US: Northwestern University Press.

Taylor, Phillip M. 2011. War Correspondents. *The Encyclopedia of War.* Published online November. Blackwell Publishing.

Thussu, Daya Kishan, and Des Freedman. 2003. *War and the Media: Reporting Conflict 24/7.* London & Thousand Oaks, CA: SAGE.

Tumber, Howard, and Frank Webster. 2006. *Journalists under Fire: Information War and Journalistic Practices.* London & Thousand Oaks: SAGE.

United Nations Resolution 2222. 2015. 7450th Meeting. May 27. See http://www.un.org/press/en/2015/sc11908.doc.htm. Accessed March 20, 2016.

United Nations Resolution A/RES/68/163. 2013. See http://www.un.org/en/events/journalists/. Accessed March 20, 2016.

Williams, Kevin. 2012. "War Correspondents as Sources for History: Problems and Possibilities in Journalism Historiography." *Media History* 18(3–4): 341–360.

Some Helpful Resources for Journalists

Journalism Support Groups

Frontline Defenders

General email – info@frontlinedefenders.org
General phone – +353 (0)1 212 3750
Web address – www.frontlinedefenders.org

International News Safety Institute

Director – Hannah Storm – hannah.storm@newssafety.org
Mobile – +44 7766 814274
Web address – www.newssafety.org

RISC (Reporters Instructed in Saving Colleagues)

Deputy director – Lily Hindy – lhindy@risctraining.org
General phone – none
Web address – risctraining.org

Dart Center for Journalism and Trauma

Executive director – Bruce Shapiro – bruce.shapiro@dartcenter.org
General phone – none
Web address – dartcenter.org

Free Press Unlimited

Contact person – Leon Williams – info@freepressunlimited.org
General phone – +31 20 8000 400
Web address – www.freepressunlimited.org

International Women's Media Foundation

Executive director – Elisa Lees Munoz
General phone – +1 (202) 496 1992
Web address – www.iwmf.org

IREX

Media person – Jennifer Nevin – jnevin@irex.org
General phone – +1 (202) 628 8188 x214
Web address – www.irex.org

Open Society Foundation

General phone – +1 (212) 548 0600
Executive director – James Goldston
Web address – www.opensocietyfoundations.org

The Rory Peck Trust

Email – info@rorypecktrust.org
General phone – +44 (0) 203 219 7860
Web address – rorypecktrust.org

UNESCO

General phone – +33 (0) 1 45 68 17 06
Web address – en.unesco.org

Article 19

Email address – communications@article19.org
General phone – +44 (0) 20 7324 2510
Web address – www.article19.org

Committee to Protect Journalists

Advocacy officer – Samantha Libby – slibby@cpj.org
General phone – +1 (212) 300-9032
Web address – www.cpj.org

Electronic Frontier Foundation

Media relations director – Rebecca Jeschke – rebecca@eff.org
General phone – +1 (415) 436 9333 x125
Web address – www.eff.org

International Freedom of Exchange

IFEX is a Toronto-based nonprofit network of some 95 independent organizations founded in Montréal in 1992. IFEX was established to create a coordinated mechanism to rapidly expose free expression violations around the world.
Media enquiries – media@ifex.org
General phone – none
Web address – www.ifex.org

International Press Institute

Executive director – Alison Bethel Mckenzie
General email – ipi@freemedia.at
General phone – +43 1 512 90 11
Web address – www.freemedia.at

Reporters Without Borders

Press and communications – presse@rsf.org
General phone – +33 (0) 1 44 83 84 56
Web address – en.rsf.org

Global Voices

Executive director – Ivan Sigal – ivan@globalvoices.org
General phone – none
Web address – globalvoices.org

Public Insight Network

PIN bureau chief – Rebecca Blatt – Rebecca.Blatt@asu.edu
General phone – none
Web address – www.publicinsightnetwork.org

World Pulse

General phone – +1 (503) 331 3900
Web address – www.worldpulse.com

Hostile Training Companies

AKE

General phone – none
Web address – www.akegroup.com

Centurion

General phone – +44 1637 873661
Web address – www.centurionsafety.net

CPJ

General phone – +1 (212) 300–9032
Web address – www.cpj.org
https://www.cpj.org/reports/2012/04/journalist-security-guide.php

Secure Transmission

Freedom of the Press Foundation

General phone – +1 (415) 767 5566
Web address – freedom.press

Electronic Frontier Foundation

General phone – +1 (415) 436 9333
Web address – www.eff.org

Internet Archive

General phone – +1 (415) 561 6767
Web address – archive.org

Onion Share

General phone – none
Web address – onionshare.org

Open Archive

General phone – none
Web address – www.openarchives.org

Open Whisper System

General phone – none
Web address – whispersystems.org

Index

Taylor & Francis eBooks

Helping you to choose the right eBooks for your Library

Add Routledge titles to your library's digital collection today. Taylor and Francis ebooks contains over 50,000 titles in the Humanities, Social Sciences, Behavioural Sciences, Built Environment and Law.

Choose from a range of subject packages or create your own!

Benefits for you

>> Free MARC records
>> COUNTER-compliant usage statistics
>> Flexible purchase and pricing options
>> All titles DRM-free.

Benefits for your user

>> Off-site, anytime access via Athens or referring URL
>> Print or copy pages or chapters
>> Full content search
>> Bookmark, highlight and annotate text
>> Access to thousands of pages of quality research at the click of a button.

REQUEST YOUR **FREE** INSTITUTIONAL TRIAL TODAY

Free Trials Available
We offer free trials to qualifying academic, corporate and government customers.

eCollections – Choose from over 30 subject eCollections, including:

Archaeology	Language Learning
Architecture	Law
Asian Studies	Literature
Business & Management	Media & Communication
Classical Studies	Middle East Studies
Construction	Music
Creative & Media Arts	Philosophy
Criminology & Criminal Justice	Planning
Economics	Politics
Education	Psychology & Mental Health
Energy	Religion
Engineering	Security
English Language & Linguistics	Social Work
Environment & Sustainability	Sociology
Geography	Sport
Health Studies	Theatre & Performance
History	Tourism, Hospitality & Events

For more information, pricing enquiries or to order a free trial, please contact your local sales team: www.tandfebooks.com/page/sales